STAFF SUPERVISION MADE EASY

SCOTT D. HUTTON, PH.D.

FOUNDED 1870

American Correctional Association
Lanham, MD

American Correctional Association Staff

Cover design by Michael Selby. Image provided by © 1994 PhotoDisc, Inc.

Printed in the United States of America by Graphic Communications, Inc.,
    Upper Marlboro, MD.

ISBN 1-56991-093-6

This publication may be ordered from:
American Correctional Association
4380 Forbes Boulevard
Lanham, Maryland 20706-4322
1-800-222-5646

For information on publications and videos available from ACA, contact our
worldwide web home page at: http://www.corrections.com/aca.

Library of Congress Cataloging-in-Publication Data

Hutton, Scott D.
    Staff supervision made easy / Scott D. Hutton
        p. cm.
    Includes bibliographical references (p.).
    ISBN 1-56991-093-6 (pbk.)
    1. Supervision of employees. 2. Correctional personnel.
    I. Title.
    HF5549.12H88 1998
    365'.068'3—dc21   98-18872
                                                               CIP

TABLE OF CONTENTS

FOREWORD

Proper supervision in a correctional setting sets the tone for the smooth running of the facility or operation and the satisfaction of the staff who work there. Job satisfaction may be measured by employees' longevity in their position and lack of workers' compensation complaints and fewer sick days than other sites of comparable size.

As the author points out, supervision is something that is learned. It is not an inbred trait that suddenly blooms when one becomes a supervisor. Instead, supervision is "getting work done through other people by setting goals, giving direction, and providing feedback." The goals that are set must be realistic and supervisors must set the tone for the institution and those they supervise.

Hutton reminds us that as supervisors, our employees are consenting adults. Each employee chose to take the job and stay. While it is not the supervisor's job to make employees work, the supervisor is obligated to explain the job to each employee and provide feedback on that employee's performance in the job. In a reader-friendly way, Hutton explains how to do this. Both new supervisors and those old-hands in the field will gain fresh insights and after reading this work will be able to administer discipline, respond to grievances, and conduct employee performance evaluations with greater equanimity and ease than before.

At our 1995 Winter Conference in Dallas, Texas, ACA's Delegate Assembly renewed the Public Correctional Policy on Correctional Staff Recruitment and Development. In its introduction, the policy states, "Knowledgeable, highly skilled, motivated, and professional correctional personnel are essential to fulfill the purpose of corrections effectively. Professionalism is achieved through structured programs of recruitment and enhancement of the employee's skills, knowledge, insight and understanding of the corrections process." The policy continues: . . . "The education, recruitment, orientation, supervision, compensation, training, retention and advancement of correctional staff must receive full support from the executive, judicial and legislative branches of government. To achieve this, correctional agencies should: select, promote and retain staff in accordance with valid job-related procedures that emphasize merit and technical competence."

Mr. Hutton explains how supervisors can follow these guidelines. He does not suggest a one-size supervision fits all approach. Rather, he explains how supervisors can determine their own leadership styles and use these to the best advantage of the organization.

In addition to this work, the American Correctional Association offers a broad spectrum of publications and materials on management and leadership issues. We invite you to visit our webpage and learn more about ACA: www.corrections.com/aca.org, or call us for more information on professional development opportunities at 1-800-ACA-JOIN.

James A. Gondles, Jr.
Executive Director
American Correctional Association

Introduction

Congratulations! You have just been promoted to a supervisory position. Now what? What is a supervisor? What does a supervisor do? Do you have what it takes to be a supervisor? How do you supervise employees who used to be your coworkers, peers, and perhaps friends? These may be some of the many questions that are going through your mind as a newly promoted supervisor.

These questions, which are "new supervisor's fears," are, indeed, legitimate and need to be addressed quickly—before a person can become an effective and efficient supervisor.

Supervisors have changed over the years, but the basic aspects of effective supervision have not. The key to becoming an efficient supervisor is to know, understand, practice, and use the basic aspects of supervision. Once you understand and apply the basics, you will gain confidence and improve your competence.

Supervisors, contrary to popular belief, are not "born;" rather, they are "made." Good supervisors are "made" by their personal and professional desire to excel and by taking the time to learn the basics of supervision. Then, they continually must engage in a learning process to enable them to improve their supervisory skills.

Since the beginning of time, humans have lived and worked together to accomplish certain mutual goals. In so doing, they saw the need for someone to direct the actions of others so that these goals were obtained. Someone needed to take charge, or, supervise.

In prehistoric days, leaders were oftentimes either the oldest or the strongest among their group. For example, when prehistoric people needed to eat, they hunted for their food. There were several jobs involved with hunting. Someone needed to spot the prey; someone needed to chase the prey to a designated area; someone needed to kill the prey; someone needed to clean or prepare the prey; and someone needed to make clothes out of the prey's hide. To accomplish these tasks, a supervisor needed to assign these jobs to the right people who could perform them properly. To do this, the supervisor needed to know the strengths and weaknesses of people to assign them the proper job so that they could accomplish the common goal: getting food to eat and making clothing.

Supervisors from the primitive days until now have changed, but some of the basic aspects of supervision have not. The previous example shows some of the aspects of supervision that have not changed: knowing the strengths and weaknesses of those you supervise, assigning the right person to the right job, making sure that the job gets done right, and then as the supervisor, providing positive feedback and rewards for job performance.

One of the earliest needs for formal supervision of people existed in the military. Two distinct groups made up an army. There were the educated group or elite who managed the army, and there were the uneducated masses who were the foot soldiers. To get the troops to follow army plans and regulations, they needed overseers. Upper management chose the biggest and strongest of the troops and elevated them to "supervisory positions." They oversaw the work of others with threats and force, and the system worked.

While the brute-force style of leadership apparently worked in the early military, it has no place in today's workforce. Unfortunately, there are still those supervisors who think that they must lead by brute force, intimidation, and other archaic methods that have proven to be of no benefit.

Because of supervisors leading by intimidation, policies, procedures, and supervisory qualifications have been implemented in most, if not all, workplaces today. Such qualifications include the abilities to communicate effectively, solve problems, and to provide positive reinforcement. With today's better educated employees taking entry-level positions in the job market, supervisors must enhance their supervisory skills. Today's employees will not tolerate the supervisory styles of the supervisors from yesteryear.

Training

Additionally, with technological advances, increased employee rights, and unionization of the workforce, supervisory training is of the utmost importance for contemporary newly promoted supervisors. The old adage of "you're promoted, now get out there and supervise" will not work today. In fact, administrators who continue to adhere to that adage will find themselves with disgruntled employees and incompetent supervisors.

Administrators are doing themselves, their supervisors, and their line staff a disservice by not properly training newly promoted supervisors before they actually assume a supervisory role. Inadequate training, or the absence of training, places the administrator, and sometimes the supervisor, in a legally indefensible situation. Therefore, proper training of supervisors is not only good practice but necessary to avoid or mitigate costly legal suits. Though the agency or employer should offer supervisory training, if this does not occur, newly promoted supervisors should exert the initiative to obtain the necessary training.

This book is a first step. Its purpose is to give newly promoted supervisors the basics to do their job properly, effectively, and efficiently. Although this book is written primarily for newly promoted supervisors, seasoned supervisors, middle managers, and agency administrators might find its information useful as a refresher course. Each chapter in this book discusses integral aspects of supervisors' jobs. After reading this book, the newly promoted supervisor should be equipped to supervise people with more efficiency and better results than previously.

This book, however, is just the beginning of what should be an ongoing educational process. To become and remain top-notch, supervisors continually will have to assess their supervisory skills, keep current on supervisory issues, and read publications pertaining to corrections and their particular niche in this field. Supervision is an ongoing process that requires dedicated people who are willing to learn and improve.

The author discusses the various aspects of supervision, such as: determining what one's supervisory style is, defining supervision, developing skills needed for effective supervision, dealing with employee personnel issues, judging how to properly administer discipline, learning how to conduct employee performance evaluations, appreciating the importance of training, and understanding the various laws that affect the employees supervised.

1 KNOW YOUR LEADERSHIP STYLE

Now that you have been promoted to a supervisory position and have agreed to accept the responsibilities that are inherent with that role, it is time to learn just what a supervisor does. Supervising other people is no easy task. It requires skill, tact, and knowledge—all of which can be learned.

Supervisory skills, once learned, must be practiced. Additionally, good supervisors continually are seeking ways to improve their supervisory skills. To improve their skills, supervisors first must determine what their supervisory style is.

Supervision Defined

Supervision can be defined as getting work done through other people (American Correctional Association, 1991a). It also can be defined as influencing others to do what the leader wants them to do (Mondy, Sharplin, and Premeaux, 1991). For the purpose of this discussion, we will define supervision as getting work done through other people by setting goals, giving direction, and providing feedback.

The first two definitions of supervision lack an integral aspect of a supervisor's responsibility. It is not enough to get the job done, but, the job must be done right. To get the job done right, individuals must know what is expected of them and how well they did. That is why it is important to add to the definition of supervision, setting goals, giving directions, and providing feedback. Once all of these aspects are combined, we have a strong working definition of supervision.

The goal of good supervision is to create a climate in the work site that encourages and rewards subordinates. This is done through positive people management. Positive people management means providing respect, encouragement, and help (American Correctional Association, 1991b).

No two supervisors are alike; therefore, most supervisors will have their own style of supervising. However, several supervisory styles appear to be the most common in the workplace. We now will look at some of the more common styles of supervision. There is not necessarily a "right" or "wrong" style of supervision. Often, individuals' supervisory styles change from time to time. It is also possible, and sometimes necessary, for your supervisory style to change depending on the particular situation.

Remember, effective supervisors not only will be cognizant of various supervisory styles, but also will practice the style(s) with which they are most comfortable. Very quickly, once they assume the role of supervisor, they will discover that the more leadership styles they can display, the better off they will be. The key to being an effective supervisor is to discover the supervisory styles that are most compatible with your personality traits and to practice the various skills associated with those supervisory styles.

Leadership Styles

According to Mondy et al. (1991), there are four leadership styles:

1. Autocratic

2. Participative

3. Democratic

4. Laissez-faire

Autocratic Leader

An autocratic leader tells subordinates what to do and expects these things to be done without question (Mondy et al., 1991). In this style of leadership, the supervisor sets the goals, tells the subordinates what to do, and then waits for the job to get done. There is no room for discussion and little opportunity for feedback. Most of the feedback the subordinates receive would be negative. This style of leadership does not allow for the workers to try and do the job in a more efficient manner. They do it the way they are told.

The autocratic style of leadership appears to be negative. However, in certain situations, this style leadership is appropriate. For example, in an emergency situation, it is necessary for the leader to take control and tell others what to do to get the job done properly. In a prison, where a major disturbance is taking place and lives are at stake, an autocratic leader may be required.

As a general rule, however, autocratic leaders normally have employees with low morale, low ambition, and the employees do enough work just to "get by." Employees have no reason to attempt to excel under this style of leadership, because the autocratic leader expects outstanding job performance to be the rule, not the exception.

Participative Leader

A participative leader is a leader who involves subordinates in decision making, but may retain the final authority to make the decision (Mondy, Sharplin, and Premeaux, 1991). In this style of leadership, the supervisor will have meetings with subordinates and get their input in order to set goals and make decisions that could affect the employees. Furthermore, the leader will keep subordinates informed concerning the decision.

If a supervisor chooses to use this style of leadership, it is important to know that not all employees want to be involved in the decision-making process. Some employees like to have the decisions made for them and the goals set for them, because they view this as a supervisor's job.

The participative style of leadership may backfire on new supervisors. New supervisors want to do what is right, and sometimes it is difficult to make a tough decision. Therefore, they will try to get the input of subordinates. While this open-minded approach to supervision is commended by most administrators, line staff (especially those who wanted to get promoted and did not) oftentimes view this as a sign of weakness in the new supervisor. Comments such as "he just got promoted and has to ask us how to make a decision" may be prevalent.

The participative style of leadership may be a very positive style if used properly. For example, employees who are high achievers and want to move up the career ladder will appreciate this style of leadership. They will be pleased that they are being asked to lend their knowledge and expertise in the decision-making process. The participative style of leadership works for supervisors whose subordinates view them as competent. If subordinates view their supervisors as incompetent, this leadership style will backfire and cause the supervisor numerous problems.

A final drawback of this style of leadership is that if the employees are involved in the decision-making process and the decision that they collectively make is not the decision that the supervisor ultimately makes, the employees involved may view their time invested in this decision-making process as wasted and unimportant. Therefore, it is imperative that leaders who use the participative approach to supervision remind staff that their input is used to "help" make decisions, not necessarily used to "make" the decision. The supervisor retains the right and responsibility to make the final decision.

For example, if you want to use the participative style of leadership to come up with a solution to the problem of low morale, you would assemble a group of employees, preferably some from each shift, and state the problem to them. "It has been brought to my attention that we have been experiencing personnel problems that are associated with low morale. This committee's responsibility is to generate some ideas on how we can improve the morale of our employees. Once you generate some ideas, I will meet with you and we will discuss the pro's and con's of each idea. The idea(s) that are acceptable, we will take steps to implement. I need your input to help me with this problem; however, I may or may not use your ideas in their entirety."

Democratic Leader

A democratic leader is a person who tries to do what the majority of subordinates desire (Mondy, Sharplin, and Premeaux, 1991). The leadership characteristics of the participative and democratic leader are closely intertwined. In this style of leadership, teams and/or ad-hoc committees are assigned certain tasks to perform. Once they make a decision, they will garner comments and suggestions from other employees. Once all of this is accomplished, the team or ad-hoc committee will forward their recommendation to the administrator for implementation.

In a democratic style of leadership, the supervisor has relinquished the decision making to a particular team or ad-hoc committee. The team or ad-hoc committee then is empowered to make a suggestion on the final decision to the administrator, and the decision, then, is implemented.

This style of leadership works well with employees who are highly motivated and goal oriented. The employees feel a sense of satisfaction and accomplishment in knowing that they were responsible for making a decision that affected their job.

The key to using this style of leadership properly is to make sure that the team or ad-hoc committee selected consists of highly motivated staff members and that they have a keen understanding of the importance of their decision and the possible ramifications it could have. Using this style of leadership normally increases the morale, job satisfaction, and work output from employees. For example, using a democratic style of leadership for a low morale problem, your instructions to the committee might be phrased this way: "This committee's responsibility is to come up with ways that we can improve the morale of our staff. You are empowered to generate and implement ways to accomplish this. Once you generate ideas, inform me first so that your ideas can be implemented. Keep in mind, we are only able to spend "x" amount of dollars on this endeavor."

The adverse affect of this style of leadership is similar to the negative affect of the participative leadership style, which is, if the committee is told they have the power to implement the decision, make sure they are allowed to do so. Failure to allow them to implement their idea(s) may cause morale problems.

Laissez-faire Leader

The laissez-faire leader is uninvolved in the work of the unit (Mondy, Sharplin, and Premeaux, 1991). This is a hands-off leader. This type of leader expects things to go as planned. Furthermore, this type of leader expects employees to be experts in their chosen field, highly motivated, and in need of no supervision.

Leaders of this type have no interest in their job or employees. They expect the job to get done, and they do not want to be bothered by anyone.

This type of leadership would work with exceptional employees who are indeed highly motivated, extremely knowledgeable, and trustworthy. But, for the typical workplace, this leadership style will not work. For example, this type of leader would say, "Here is your job description, now do your job." Supervisors of this type would not check up on the employees because they would expect the job to be done, and done right. The employees would lack any feedback concerning their job performance and would not know where they needed to improve nor how to improve. In fact, this type of leader may not last long in a typical correctional environment.

This type of supervisory style can work only under extreme circumstances. Employees working for this type of supervisor will enjoy empowerment at its highest level. Those employees who are not competent enough to handle the empowerment will experience extreme stress and a sense of being unorganized. However, most employees will not be able to work for this type of supervisor mainly because they are used to having a supervisor show some interest in the job and set goals for them to obtain.

Experienced Leaders

The experienced leader uses many complex supervision behaviors and supervisory styles. These leadership styles can range from highly leader-centered to highly group-centered.

Managerial Grid

Robert R. Blake and Jane S. Marton developed another popular approach to categorizing various supervisory styles. Their "managerial grid" (Heyel, 1973) is an extension of McGregor's Theory X and Theory Y.

In McGregor's book, *The Human Side of Enterprise*, he set forth six assumptions about industrial behavior, contrasting them with the traditional view, which he termed "Theory X" (McGregor, 1960). He called his new assumptions on industrial behavior "Theory Y." The assumptions concerning Theory Y as contrasted to Theory X are enumerated next:

1. The expenditure of physical and mental effort is as natural as play or rest. This is contrasted with Theory X which contends that the average human beings have an inherent dislike of work and will avoid it if they can.

2. People will exercise self-direction and self-control for objectives to which they are committed. This is contrasted with Theory X, which states that most people must be coerced, controlled, directed, and threatened with punishment to get them to put forth adequate effort toward the achievement of organizational objectives.

3. Commitment to objectives is a function of the rewards associated with their achievement. The most significant of such rewards, for example, the satisfaction of ego and self-actualization needs, can be direct products of effort directed toward organizational objectives.

4. The average human being learns, under proper conditions, not only to accept but to seek responsibility. This is contrasted with Theory X, which states that the average human being prefers to be directed, wishes to avoid responsibility, has relatively little ambition and wants security above all.

5. The capacity to exercise a relatively high degree of imagination, ingenuity, and creativity in the solution of organizational problems is widely distributed, not narrowly distributed in the population (as Theory X contends).

6. According to Theory Y, under the conditions of modern industrial life, the intellectual potentialities of the average human being are only partially realized (Heyel, 1973).

Styles of Management

Using the basic assumptions of McGregor's theory, Heyel delineated, on a managerial grid, five distinct supervisory styles of management (1973).

The managerial grid is a series of questions that the managers answer to give a self-appraisal of their management style (Blake and Morton, 1964). Once the managers complete their answers and tally their scores, the managers can "plot" their scores on a grid, which indicates their leadership style.

The leadership styles are contrasted by a concern for people and a concern for production. The five styles of leadership according to the managerial grid include the following:

1. *Impoverished Management.* In this style of management, there is minimum exertion of effort to get the required work done. Managers with this leadership style have little concern for either people or production.

2. *Authority-Obedience.* In this style of management, the efficiency in operations results from arranging conditions of work in such a way that human elements interfere to a minimum degree. The manager stresses operating efficiently through strict controls. Managers exhibiting this style of leadership have a high concern for production and a low concern for people.

3. *Country Club Management.* In this style of management, thoughtful attention to the needs of people for satisfying relationships leads to a comfortable, friendly organizational atmosphere and work tempo. This type of manager is thoughtful, comfortable, and friendly, and has a high concern for people and a low concern for production.

4. *Organization-type Management.* In this style of management, adequate organizational performance is possible through balancing the necessity to get work out while maintaining morale of the people at a satisfactory level. This type of manager attempts to balance and trade off concern for work in exchange for a satisfactory level of morale. This type of leader is a compromiser who has a moderate concern for people and a moderate concern for production.

5. *Team Management.* In this style of management, work accomplishment is a result of committed people. Employees have an interdependence through a "common stake" in the organization's purpose, which leads to relationships of trust and respect. This type of manager seeks high output through committed people. This output is achieved through mutual

trust, respect, and a realization of interdependence. This type of manager has a high concern for people and a high concern for production (Mondy, Sharplin, and Premeaux, 1991).

We have examined various supervisory styles. No one style is the right style for all situations. Supervisors will want to know and practice two or three of these styles with which they feel most comfortable. Remember, there is no right or wrong supervisory style. Supervisory styles are an extension of the manager and can change depending upon the situation and/or the people being supervised.

Factors Influencing Supervisory Styles

Factors that influence supervisory styles may be inherent in the leader, in the group, and in the situation. Each of these factors can help determine the supervisory style most effective for each leader.

The factors that can influence a supervisor's styles are enumerated next:

1. *Factors in the leader.* Depending upon one's background, knowledge, and experience, each supervisor will perceive leadership problems in a unique way. The leader's value system also will play a role in the leadership style one chooses. Also, the leader's confidence, or lack of confidence, in the group one is supervising could affect one's supervisory style. Finally, one's own inclinations will play a role, as well.

2. *Factors in the group.* Before deciding how to exercise leadership, the leader also should consider a number of forces that are affecting the group's behavior, such as the group member's ages, gender, education level, interest in the job, length of time on the job, job skills, and so forth. Additionally, each member of the group is influenced by many personality variables. The better the supervisor understands these factors, the more accurately the supervisor can determine how to help members of the group to act effectively. Generally speaking, supervisors can provide their group of subordinates the greatest freedom if these employees exhibit a need for independence, are ready to assume responsibility, have a tolerance for ambiguity, have a high level of interest, understand goals, and have adequate levels of knowledge and experience.

3. *Factors in the situation.* In addition to the forces which exist in the supervisor and in the group, certain characteristics of the general situation also will affect the leader's supervisory style. Some of these factors include:

the type of organization, the group's effectiveness, the problem itself, and the pressure of time (American Correctional Association, 1991).

Discovering Your Supervisory Style

To become an effective supervisor, one must know what one's supervisory style is and consciously practice it. It also is necessary to be cognizant of the capabilities and abilities of your assigned staff members. Individuals also will need to be aware of the factors that can influence their supervisory style. Furthermore, the supervisor should be aware of the fact that supervising people is an ongoing learning process. Thus, supervisors who want to excel will strive continually to better themselves through continuing education in the field of supervision and in corrections.

Finally, once you do discover your leadership style, practice it. To be a good supervisor, one must be consistent, fair, and consistently fair. The supervisor must lead subordinate personnel by setting a good example. Everyone leads by example, some by good example, some by bad example. Be the good-example supervisor who others will want to follow.

Influence Others to Want to Follow

Leaders in contemporary organizations influence others to want to follow. They do this by creating an organizational situation in which committed, self-confident people work in exciting jobs that enhance their follower's self-esteem. This is the role of modern leaders and the goal that should drive your leadership behavior. The goal contains four key elements: creating commitment, creating self-confidence, creating exciting jobs, and creating self-esteem (Lynch, 1993).

Be Yourself

Do not attempt to be someone who you are not. Do not try to be a forceful leader if your style is that of a participative leader. Each leadership style has its benefits.

Learn from Others

Do not be afraid to talk with other supervisors and learn from them. Remember, all of the seasoned supervisors were once new supervisors, not unlike yourself. The problems they encountered may be similar to the ones you encounter. Do not be afraid to ask for their advice and guidance. You will discover that a seasoned supervisor could be your best ally and teacher.

You will be in the learning phase of your new position for a few months. Do not set yourself up for failure by expecting to know all that there is to know about supervision. Supervision is an ongoing process. Also, do not be afraid to learn from whatever mistakes that you might make as a new supervisor. Use your experiences, and the experiences of your cosupervisors, as learning tools. Learn from what did not go right and correct it so that you will not make the same mistake again. Once you master your supervisory style, supervising will be one of the best experiences of your career.

In the next chapter, we will examine the various traits and skills of an effective supervisor.

2 TRAITS, SKILLS, AND PRINCIPLES OF EFFECTIVE SUPERVISION

Just as there are various supervisory styles, there also are various supervisory traits, skills, and principles that an efficient supervisor will want to learn. The traits, skills, and principles that are discussed are not intended to be an all-inclusive list. However, they are some of the more important traits, skills, and principles that will help you be an effective supervisor.

In many ways, supervising people is a very easy job. As long as you practice a supervisory style with which you are comfortable and follow the basic assumptions concerning supervision that are listed next, you should enjoy your new role as a supervisor.

According to Raddle (1981), when you understand certain supervisory assumptions, your job of supervising becomes easy, or at least easier. They are as follows:

1. Your employees are consenting adults. Each employee chose to take the job and stay. It is not your job to make your employees work.

2. Employee responsibility to the organization begins with the hiring interview. Both the interviewer and the applicant have a responsibility to match real ability, potential, and willingness to learn with the actual requirements of the job.

3. Your employees are under contract with the organization. By contract, they are entitled to remuneration and benefits in return for the specific performance of job activities and responsibilities assigned to them.

4. When you enter an organization under an employment contract, you become "personnel." The focus or basis for the supervisor-employee relationship is the work, which must continue to be held primary and foremost to sustain the mission of the organization and the organization itself.

5. In most cases, you will supervise intact, physically and mentally competent human beings who are capable of performing job tasks and learning new skills. They chose to work in their positions and by virtue of their employment contract, they assume responsibility to carry out the majority of the tasks assigned them within your unit.

6. Your employees share responsibility for choosing, learning, and performing their job activities, but if an employee is unsalvageable, you are not responsible.

7. A supervisor supervises task performance to get results. Task performance is the basis for the supervisor-employee relationship on the job. Know what the job requires and what resources are required to get those results. Communicate about availability of resources and objectives to employees.

8. If you try to be directly responsible for a delegated task, you really have not delegated. Rather, you have retained primary responsibility for doing that task. In other words, if you assign responsibility to another for a task, delegate it and let the employees assigned do the task. Do not tell them that they have "messed up" and then do the task yourself. If they do make mistakes, tell them what they did wrong, how to do it correctly, and let them do it. Your job is to delineate employee responsibility for tasks and to direct them to the desired results.

9. The supervisor has the responsibility of maintaining responsible job performance for each employee within the unit. The actual energy, stimulus, and choice to perform the work comes from the employee. When the employee refuses to fulfill the requirements of the job position, it is the supervisor's responsibility to fill that job position with a responsible employee.

10. Because we do not know all things, we must rely on each other to provide additional information or data. All the available facts, information,

and data regarding the organization that is held in common among employees constitute the common database, an essential element in communication and supervision. Therefore, it is imperative that you allow time in your shift meetings for feedback from the line staff and from other shift supervisors. Often, your employees will have valuable information, but they may not share it unless they are asked, or given the opportunity to do so.

11. Establishing and maintaining a common database of work-related issues and information with employees is both a major supervisory responsibility and a major employee responsibility. The importance of regular shift or roll call meetings and meetings with other supervisors cannot be overemphasized. The exchange of information that is job relevant is of paramount importance. All employees must be made aware of information that can affect their job performance, such as, unruly inmates, rumors of potential problems in a certain housing area, and other issues. By sharing available, accurate, and current information on work responsibilities and organization realities, stress is reduced. Giving and getting input on the common database is a vital and continuing communication practice for meeting organizational goals. Note: this information may exist in both oral and/or written form as well as on a computer.

12. Reality never lets you down. Only your own expectations, distortions, and demands on reality let you down (Raddle, 1981). In other words, do not set yourself up for failure because you put unreasonable demands on yourself or your employees. Know your limitations and the limitations of your employees.

Many supervisors, especially new supervisors, oftentimes assume more responsibility than the job entails. Supervisors may think that the entire success or failure of a project rests on their shoulders and that they must force their employees to get the job done. While the ultimate success or failure is the responsibility of the supervisor, the supervisor only can do so much.

By following these assumptions concerning supervision, one readily can observe that assigning the correct person to do the right job is of paramount importance. Supervisors have to learn that not all employees are capable of performing all job functions, nor are employees all capable of performing their job functions with the same precision or speed. Additionally, a supervisor cannot make a person work. Supervisors will need to know the strengths and weaknesses of their employees so they can make the right job assignments and achieve the established goal.

LEAD Principles

Another method used to lead employees is referred to as the LEAD principles. The LEAD principles, according to Carlisle and Murphy (1986) include:

L —*Listen and respond with concern and interest. Concern* means the supervisor recognizes the employee's feelings—is the employee upset, happy, frustrated, angry, bored, and so forth? *Interest* means the supervisor listens carefully enough to restate the content of what the employee says. A true listening response includes both feeling and content. Finally, listening responses avoid words like "but" or "however" because these words negate what the employee says and imply that the supervisor's words are more important. Consider using the words "and" and "instead" or pause before sharing an alternative idea.

E —Encourage and praise employees. The supervisor must encourage employees by mentioning each employee's strengths. As the employees do well, supervisors must give very specific praise. The praise must be honest and sincere or it will be rejected. Never say anything that demeans an employee's skills, abilities, or integrity.

A —Ask for the employee's help. This principle is very important to ensuring participation, to fostering commitment, and to building the employee's self-image. Asking an employee for help makes the employee feel important. Asking for help might lead to idea generation, priority setting, or some related activity.

D —Decide on specific actions. A leader is, by definition, an action-oriented individual. Leaders get things done. If one method fails, the supervisor needs to implement another one. Make decisions quickly, then act, and get employees involved (Carlisle and Murphy, 1986).

Use of the LEAD principles should assist supervisors in developing necessary skills to better supervise and motivate their employees. Furthermore, the LEAD principles foster a positive work atmosphere characterized by employees who are willing to approach their supervisors with problems, concerns, and suggestions.

Eight Leadership Principles

Another management guru, Rosen (1996), has identified eight principles for leading people that are essential for effective supervision. They include the following:

1. *Vision.* Leaders see the whole picture and articulate that broad perspective with others. By doing so, leaders create a common purpose that mobilizes people and coordinates their efforts into a single, coherent, agile enterprise.

2. *Trust.* Without trust, vision becomes an empty slogan. Trust binds people together to create a strong, resilient organization. To build trust, leaders are predictable, and they share information and power. Their goal is a culture of candor.

3. *Participation.* The energy of an organization is the participation and effort of its people. The leader's challenge is to unleash and focus this energy, inspiring people at every level of the enterprise to pitch in with their minds and hearts.

4. *Learning.* Leaders need a deep understanding of themselves. They must know their strengths and shortcomings, a process which requires a life-long discovery, and they must be able to adapt to new circumstances.

5. *Diversity.* Successful leaders know the power of diversity and the poison of prejudice. They understand their own biases, and they actively cultivate an appreciation of the positive aspects of people's differences. In their organizations, they insist on a culture of mutual respect (American Correctional Association, 1993).

6. *Creativity.* In a world where smart solutions should outpace excessive work, creativity is crucial. Leaders pay close attention to people's talents, leaning on their strengths, and managing around their weaknesses. They encourage independent, challenging thinking, and they invest in technologies that improve the efforts of their people.

7. *Integrity.* Leaders must stand for something. As public citizens and private individuals, leaders should know what is important in life and act by deep-seated principles. As public citizens, leaders must perform their job in a manner to bring noteworthy credit to themselves and their agencies. And, as private citizens, especially as corrections professionals, it is important for them to obey the law and not have a double standard. Every wise leader has a moral compass, a sense of right and wrong. Good leaders understand that good ethics is good business. In corrections, good ethics and good business mean a well-run organization operating by established policies and within budgetary constraints.

8. *Community.* Community requires mutual commitment, and it inspires the highest performance. It is human nature to go the extra mile for one's neighbors and fellow citizens. A mature leader stresses the organization's responsibility to the surrounding areas (Rosen, 1996).

The eight principles of effective leadership are attainable. In fact, it would be difficult to be an effective leader without adhering to these principles. Yet, none of these principles is something that is inherent within supervisors. Rather, each principle can be learned. Recall our starting observation, good supervisors can be "taught" to be good supervisors, they are not "born" that way.

Good Leaders Are Like Coaches

Some equate supervising people to the role of a coach. What makes a coach successful? Undoubtedly, your list of success factors for coaches will include the following: using effective planning skills, desiring to get ahead, being willing to take creative risks, feeling self-confident in their abilities and in the abilities of their team, wanting to take responsibility, using problem solving, giving credit where credit is due, and taking responsibility when something goes wrong. If you ever have listened to a postgame interview with a coach of a winning team, you will see most of these characteristics exhibited. The good coaches (even those on the losing teams) will exhibit these same characteristics. If you think about it, a good supervisor is just like a coach and should exhibit the same characteristics.

- Use effective planning skills

- Have a desire to get ahead

- Be willing to take creative risks

- Feel self-confident in your own, as well as your team's abilities

- Want to take responsibility

- Use problem solving skills

- Give credit where credit is due

- Take responsibility when something goes wrong

Mondy (1991) offers the following tips to help ensure success as a supervisor:

1. *Gather influence.* Harsh as this may sound, the amount of influence managers have over subordinates is determined largely by the manager's influence outside the unit.

2. *Lead through example.* Employees often use the manager as a role model in deciding what is right or wrong.

3. *Be specific.* Make sure that your people know what you want done.

4. *Be competent, then confident.* Once you know the job well, you will have confidence. Acting confident without knowing the job is cockiness.

5. *Look like a leader.* Dress appropriately for a manager in your organization.

6. *Sound like a leader.* When you issue an order, say what you mean and mean what you say.

7. *Be objective.* Lead your workers in a positive direction that is fair to them, to you, and to the organization.

8. *Do not pass on a directive from upper management with an apology.* Some supervisors accept a directive from upper management without question and then criticize the directive while transmitting it to subordinates. Remember, to your workers, you are management. The spirit in which the supervisor passes on a directive will have a major impact on how the job is done.

9. *Do not blindly follow directives that you know are incorrect.* Question them. Make sure that you do what is legally, ethically, and morally correct (Mondy et al., 1991).

Implementing These Tips

To implement these nine tips in corrections, the scenario would resemble something like the following: The supervisor arrives at work early and is dressed in a clean, neat uniform with shoes and brass highly shined. The supervisor reads through memos from the administration to ensure he or she has a thorough understanding of what is being said and the implication of this on staff. If the supervisor has any questions pertaining to any of the memos, he or she will find out the answers before disseminating the information to subordinate staff. As the shift members arrive for roll call, the shift supervisor will start the roll call on time and disseminate information clearly and concisely, not in an apologetic manner.

Throughout the shift, the supervisor will lead the staff by giving clear directions and positive feedback. The supervisor also will follow the established rules and not use a double standard, wherein the rules apply to line staff, but not to supervisors. Finally, the supervisor constantly will look for ways to improve himself or herself and provide opportunities for staff to do the same.

All of the skills, traits, and principles mentioned in this chapter are intended to be used as guidelines to follow and not as mandates. It will behoove a prudent supervisor to know these skills and practice them. Proper use of these skills, traits, and principles will enhance a supervisor's performance.

Management By Walking Around

However, knowing these skills is not enough. One must take the time to implement them, as well. The best way to implement these skills is by a process known as management by walking around. Management by walking around is a method of management wherein supervisors actually go out into the workplace to talk with their employees and observe the employees working.

The purpose of going out to the employees to supervise them is not to catch them doing something wrong, but rather, to catch them doing something right and to open the doors of communication between management and line staff. This author uses this method of management, and it has proven to be an effective tool. It shows employees that management does not sit behind a desk all day. It gives management hands-on knowledge of the environment and performance of employees. It opens the doors of communication, and keeps management informed about what is taking place in the workplace.

The principle behind management by walking around is closely related to the principles of Total Quality Management. Both are concerned with making sure that all aspects of an organization are running smoothly.

Total Quality Management (TQM)

W. Edward Deming, considered the father of Total Quality Management, believes that there are fourteen principles that must be followed to implement the Total Quality Management philosophy effectively. Although the Total Quality Management philosophy was developed for private industry, it is applicable to the criminal justice field, as well. The Total Quality Management principles (Sashkin, 1993) are listed next. This list is followed by an explanation of how these principles are applicable in a correctional setting.

1. *Create consistency of purpose for improvement of product and service.* There must be a continuous emphasis on quality improvement, with quality, not profit, being the primary focus.

2. *Adopt the new philosophy.* There must be a constancy of purpose, and the purpose must be shared by everyone in the company.

3. *Cease dependence on mass inspections.* Quality cannot be added on, it must be built-in from the start. Most workers want to produce products of a high caliber. Mass inspections find errors and require the worker to correct them. This means that workers are paid to make errors and correct them.

4. *End the practice of awarding business on the basis of the price tag alone.* Choice among suppliers should be based mostly on the quality of the materials they supply and on their willingness to work to improve that quality in the context of a long-term relationship. The low bidder should not be awarded a contract automatically as is the practice of many companies and governmental agencies.

5. *Improve constantly and forever the system of production and service.* Always seek out ways to improve what you are doing.

6. *Institute training.* Employees should be trained on how to do the job before they actually do it. Also, ongoing training is essential.

7. *Institute leadership.* Leaders are different from supervisors. Supervisors tell people what to do and administer rewards and discipline, as needed, to ensure compliance with orders. Leaders, however, assume that workers want to do their jobs the best way that they can. Leadership means designing a system on the basis of TQM and, constantly and consistently, modeling behavior consistent with the philosophy of TQM.

8. *Drive out fear.* In many organizations, employees are afraid to speak up to management for fear of reprisal. A climate should be fostered where employees are encouraged to point out errors and make suggestions on how to improve what is occurring without being fearful of receiving discipline.

9. *Break down barriers between staff areas.* Do not have competition between staff members. Rather, reinforce the fact that all employees within the organization are on the same team with the same goal: to make

the best quality product possible. The only competition should be between organizations, not within the organization.

10. *Eliminate slogans, exhortations, and targets for the workforce.* Deming believes that slogans and targets put people in the position of having an idea of where they want to go but no map of how to get there.

11. *Eliminate numerical quotas.* Quotas encourage people to ignore quality. The goal is to meet or exceed the quota at any cost and regardless of quality. The goal should focus on issues of quality, not on the numbers that are produced.

12. *Remove barriers to employees' pride in their work.* Deming believes that since people want to do a good job, the annual rating or merit system should be eliminated. Employees need help in overcoming work barriers and should not be penalized for barriers beyond their control that affect their work performance.

13. *Institute a vigorous program of education and improvement.* People must learn new ways of working together as teams and new behaviors that support TQM.

14. *Take action to accomplish the transformation.* Everyone in the organization must work together to implement a quality culture.

TQM in Corrections

The application of these principles in the criminal justice environment can be summed up as follows:

1. Make sure that you emphasize team goals, as opposed to individual goals. State the importance of your shift (team) getting their goals accomplished, such as lockdowns, feedings, sick call, and so forth, as opposed to one individual housing unit getting its goals completed faster than another housing unit.

2. Make sure that you, as the supervisor, are concerned with total quality, which in the correctional environment is providing the best service possible to the offenders. This will ensure the taxpayers that their tax money is being well spent.

3. Make sure that your employees are properly trained before they assume their new position. They could be assigned to a senior officer for on-the-job

training and/or required to pass a competency test after training before they work by themselves.

4. Lead by example. You need to keep abreast on the current issues that affect your agency and the criminal justice field. As the supervisor, not only must you know the rules and enforce them, you must abide by them. Furthermore, you must know how to perform the basic functions of each job description or post on your shift.

5. Foster an environment where employees believe that they can talk to you about problems, or provide suggestions on how to improve the efficiency of the agency, without fear of your reprisal. Make sure that you are approachable by your staff. Be willing to talk with them and establish a good working relationship.

6. Eliminate competition between shifts. Make sure that each shift is concerned with getting the job done right and getting it done as a team.

7. Constantly look for ways to improve your agency, yourself, and your employees.

If these principles are applied, you will see an increase in job satisfaction, morale, and productivity of staff.

Risk Management

A final aspect of supervision that needs to be examined is that of risk management. Risk management oftentimes is thought to be the sole responsibility of the top manager, or risk manager. However, risk management, especially in the correctional setting, is the responsibility of all employees.

Risk management is identifying potential harm, or risks, to the agency or department and taking the necessary steps to correct the potential harm (risks) so that they do not occur. Once the potential harm, or risk, has been identified, action must be taken to correct it and minimize its potential effect. This is where the supervisor enters. Supervisors should be cognizant of potential risks and take it upon themselves to report such risks and/or take corrective action.

In the correctional setting, there is the potential for risk on a daily basis. One should look at all aspects of the correctional setting to properly assess any potential risks. For example, the supervisor should examine the programs that are offered to inmates, the classification system to ensure that inmates are classified appropriately, the housing situation, the training of the staff, and the policies of the agency.

In other words, the supervisor should make sure that the environment is safe for staff and inmates.

If all of these aspects of the correctional environment are examined on a routine basis, you, as the supervisor, will be doing your share in helping to reduce potential risks to your agency. You also should document the results of your risk assessment so that there is a written record of it. The risk assessment should be recorded in the shift log, or, if your agency does not maintain a shift log, document the results in a memo and forward it to your supervisor.

Finally, if you discover something that is not in accordance with established policy, report it immediately to upper-level management so that appropriate corrective action may be taken. The proactive actions of a supervisor in helping to reduce the potential risks can help your agency to achieve a safe facility and reduce the likelihood of lawsuits and grievances initiated by inmates for being housed in an unsafe environment or being denied access to programs. A proactive approach also may eliminate grievances filed by employees.

Characteristics of An Effective Leader

Characteristics that are necessary to become an effective leader include the following:

1. *Good supervisors must be willing to learn.* They must have knowledge of the job that their subordinates are doing. They cannot supervise employees if they do not know what the employees are supposed to be doing in the first place.

2. *Good supervisors must be willing to improve themselves.* Supervisors must keep current on the latest supervisory skills and the ever-changing laws that affect the criminal justice field and employment law.

3. *Good supervisors must be fair.* This does not mean that you should treat all employees the same. You should, however, treat all employees in a fair manner. Do not play favorites.

4. *Good supervisors lead by setting a good example.* Subordinate personnel look up to supervisors. Attempt to be the type of supervisor who you would want to supervise you.

5. *Good supervisors are honest.* If you promise an employee something, live up to it. If you do not know the answer to your employees' questions or problems, tell them so, but find out the answer and get back to them.

6. *Good supervisors provide feedback to their employees.* Employees must know when they are doing a good job and conversely, when they are doing a bad job.

7. *Good supervisors never reprimand an employee in front of other employees.* This principle lowers employee's defensiveness. Their image is not tarnished in front of their peers. Because they are not embarrassed, they do not have to retaliate against you but can work collegially with you.

8. *Good supervisors keep accurate documentation pertaining to employees' job performance.* Accurate documentation will come in handy when you give the employees' their performance evaluations.

9. *Good supervisors understand their supervisory style and use it to their advantage.* For example, if your supervisory style is participatory, realize that fact and use that style of leadership. Do not try to become an autocratic leader.

10. *Good supervisors understand that they are an extension of the administration.* It is their duty to ensure that the administration's goals, policies, and mission are accomplished and that they support them. Never speak adversely of the administration in front of subordinate personnel.

11. *Good supervisors do not fraternize with those they supervise.* This is the quickest way to compromise the supervisor's authority.

12. *Good supervisors not only enforce the rules of the agency, but they follow them, as well.* Do not have a double standard wherein you can violate a rule with no fear of discipline and then discipline a subordinate staff member for committing the same violation.

This list of traits, skills, and principles for effective supervision discussed here may appear to be a bit overwhelming. At times, the role of a supervisor can be overwhelming, too. Yet, with practice and patience, a willing person can acquire these skills and become an effective supervisor.

In the next chapter, we will examine some of the supervisory challenges that you will encounter in your supervisory role.

3 SUPERVISORY CHALLENGES

Once new supervisors have become familiar with their supervisory styles and the various traits, skills, and principles that comprise effective supervisors, sooner or later supervisory challenges will occur. Supervisory challenges can be anything from personality conflicts among employees to recommending an employee for termination from employment.

In this chapter, we will look at some of the more common supervisory challenges and ways in which you can deal with them. The subject of discipline is covered in the following chapter.

In an "ideal" work environment, all employees love their jobs, get along with each other, follow the rules of the company, or agency, respect and obey their supervisor, and can work with little to no supervision. However, in a "realistic" work environment, there are personality conflicts among employees; some employees are only working at their current job because they cannot get a job somewhere else; employees do not always go by the rules; and they do not always respect their supervisor. But all is not lost! Supervisors can and will prevail once they are aware of potential challenges and know how to handle them.

Supervising Former Peers

One of the first challenges that practically all new supervisors face is that of supervising former peers. This challenge is compounded further if the new supervisors were especially close to one or more of their former peers. Remember, a peer is an equal, and once you are promoted, like it or not, you are no longer an equal to your former coworkers. That is not to say that you cannot still be their friend or be nice to them. It is to say, however, that you no longer will be equal to them.

Sometimes when supervisors are promoted, there is jealousy or envy among their former peers, because perhaps one of them thought that he or she should have been promoted, instead. Also, new supervisors oftentimes are "tested" by their former peers to see how they will act. Will the new supervisor let a "test" slide, or, will the new supervisor act as an extension of the administration and take the appropriate action? The way the new supervisors respond to this test from their former peers will set the tone for their new supervisory role.

If new supervisors choose to do nothing about the "test" from their former peers, they probably will remain well liked, but they will not be effective supervisors. The best way to handle former peers is discussed next.

1. Be honest with them from the moment you are promoted. You will need to convey the idea that you are now their supervisor, and you expect them to do their jobs properly.

2. Inform them that any willful disobedience, disrespect, or violations will be dealt with in accordance with the established policies and procedures.

3. Make sure that you carry through with the appropriate action if you are challenged.

It might seem harsh to have to "lay down the law" to your former peers, but human nature tells us to believe that your former peers will continue to do their jobs in the same manner as when you were their peer. Reality tells us that this is not always the case.

Finally, keep in mind that if you do not take appropriate action when you are "tested" by a former peer, then you will lose all credibility as a supervisor. Furthermore, there is a chance that you could lose your position as a supervisor if you do not take the appropriate action. If this happens, this author guarantees that one of your former peers would love to have the supervisory job that you could not handle, and they would expect you to do the job properly and obey their leadership!

Contending with Personality Types

Dealing with former peers is not the only supervisory challenge you will face. There are also various personality types with which you will have to contend. We now will examine some of the various personality types and explain what you can do to deal with them.

Bully

One particular personality type that is difficult to deal with is that of a bully. Bullies are motivated by the desire to get the job done, but only by doing it their way. Your goal in dealing with bullies is to command their respect. Bullies oftentimes think that their way is the only way, and they will do it their way until they are told to stop. In dealing with bullies, you need to hold your ground. Let them know that you are the boss, and that the job will be done according to the way you said so.

If bullies challenge you in a staff meeting, you need to tell them that you disagree with them (if you do), but give them the opportunity to explain their proposed way of doing the task. If their way of doing the task is blatantly wrong, the rest of the staff members will see that, and the bully will lose some respect that they oftentimes manage to garner.

Once bullies are put in their place, they can become productive employees. However, do not argue with bullies in front of others. This is oftentimes what they want in the first place: to get you to lose your professionalism. If an argument appears to be evident, tell bullies that you need to see them in your office at a specified time. This will show bullies, and the rest of the staff members, that you are in charge.

Back Stabber

The "back stabber" is the type of employee who is usually angry, frustrated, has low self-esteem, and likes to put you down in front of others. The best way to deal with back stabbers is to confront them. For example, if you are certain that a particular employee constantly is causing problems on the shift and putting you down in front of other staff members, you will need to have a private meeting with that employee. The employee probably will not admit to causing any of the problems about which you had heard, so you will need to point out the facts to that employee. For example, when talking in private with the back stabber, ask direct questions, such as: "I heard what you said about me, is that true? What did you mean by that?"

Make sure that you stay calm when dealing with back stabbers. Give them a chance to clarify what they said. End the conversation by stating: "The next time you have something adverse to say about me or the department, I expect you to come to me first so that we can discuss it." Make sure that employees understand that their behavior will not be tolerated. Once you discover back stabbers, they can become productive employees.

I Should Be the Supervisor-types

Another supervisory challenge is dealing with the "I should be the supervisor" people. They are employees who truly believe that they should be the supervisor instead of you. Maybe these employees were up for a promotion, but you got promoted over them.

Regardless of the case, this type of employee can be a good ally for you. The way to deal with "I should be the supervisor" people is to talk with them in private about some of their ideas. They actually might have good ideas, and they always are willing to share their "ideas" with the supervisor.

If you use one of their ideas, make sure that you give them appropriate credit. Also, ensure that you know accurate details of the subject you are talking about with this type of person, because they assuredly will express the idea that they know what they are saying! If they happen to challenge you in front of others, handle them in the same manner as the "bully" by meeting with them in private. Once the "I should be the supervisor" people are brought under control, they can be very productive employees.

People Pleasers

Another personality type is that of the "people pleasers." They have an extremely strong desire to get along with others, and they will agree with almost anything. Because it is impossible to do everything for everyone, "people pleasers" often find themselves overcommitted, and you find yourself on the short end of the results they promised you.

Your goal in dealing with "people pleasers" is to get them to make commitments and get you the results that they promised. They will always volunteer whenever you ask for volunteers. They mean well, but as we all know, it is impossible to do everything.

"People pleasers" might be difficult to discover, at first, but once you discover them (usually after they cannot get the job done as promised), you will need to talk with them in private and find out why they could not get the job done. You might want to suggest to them that maybe they were overcommitted and that they took on more than they could handle. This will allow them to save face.

Remember, "people pleasers" mean well and do not want to disappoint you. You will need to point out to them that it is impossible to continually overcommit yourself and get the job done properly. Do not continue to allow them to volunteer or overextend themselves. Set limits on them. They will appreciate it when you do set limits, since they are unwilling to set the limits themselves.

It Cannot Be Done-types

Finally, we have the "It cannot be done" people. They are employees who complain constantly and are convinced that "it cannot be done." The way to deal with people of this type is to listen to their complaints. Listen to them tell you why it cannot be done. You then will need to point out the error in their reasoning and instruct them on how to do the job.

Many times, this type is convinced that they cannot do the job because they have never been taught how to do the job properly in the first place. Once they are instructed in how to do the job, their job performance usually increases, and their complaints generally decrease. If, however, their complaining persists after they are told how to do the job and they do not it, you will need to inform them that if they have any complaints about the job, they are to voice them to you only. Instruct them that they are not to voice their complaints to coworkers and cause disruption in the workplace.

Dealing with the various personality types that employees can display is just one of the challenges that supervisors will face. Other challenges exist as well.

Counseling Employees

For some supervisors, confronting or counseling an employee can be a challenge. When you must confront or counsel an employee about a problem, you can use the following steps as a guideline:

1. *Determine if it is a problem that could lead to disciplinary action.* If it is, you will want to have another supervisor present as a witness. If it is a problem that is not likely to lead to disciplinary action, you may not want another supervisor present.

2. *Make sure that, whenever possible, the confrontation or counseling session is conducted in your office.* If you do not have an office, conduct the confrontation in an area that is not accessible to other staff members. You do not want to confront employees in front of their peers, if at all possible.

3. *Try to set a positive tone.* Try to make the employee feel at ease. Going to a supervisor's office is usually a stress-invoking event, so try to make it as stress-free as possible.

4. *Be honest and open with employees.* Tell them why they are in your office. Do not make light of the situation, or your talk could lose its effectiveness.

5. *Let the employees tell you their side of the issue.* Take notes. Make sure that you fully understand their side.

6. *Restate the issues the employees brought up.* This will give the employees a chance to "hear" their problem. Oftentimes, once employees "hear" their problem from a supervisor, they are able to understand it better.

7. *Ask employees what possible solutions or alternatives are available to help solve their problem.* Oftentimes, employees will have a proposed solution ready.

8. *Consider all of the facts.* You may not be able to decide on a solution during the confrontation. If you cannot solve the problem then, or need additional time to come up with a solution, inform employees as to when you will get back to them.

9. *Take action.* After considering all of the facts, decide on an appropriate solution. If you are unable to solve the problem, or if you have to forward the solution to your supervisor for approval, put your proposed solution in writing and forward it to the proper authority.

10. *Inform the employee of the action that you plan to take.* This can be done verbally and should be followed up in writing to the employee.

11. *Monitor the solution.* Make sure that the solution is appropriate. If it is not, you may need to modify your solution.

Problem Solving

Another challenge that supervisors are faced with on a daily basis is that of problem solving. Unfortunately, problems will not solve themselves nor will they go away. Problems must be dealt with, and dealt with properly.

The American Correctional Association (1991) has identified a seven-step problem-solving method. The seven steps include these:

1. *Identify the problem.* Gather as much information about the problem as you can and analyze the information. Make sure you properly define the problem.

2. *Generate solution ideas.* You can do this by brainstorming. The object of brainstorming is to produce an enormous number of ideas. This can be done by discussing the identified problem with other supervisors or line staff. In brainstorming, there are no right or wrong solutions. Consider all solutions initially.

3. *Then, analyze the solutions for their workability.* Go through the list of possible solutions and prioritize them from those most likely to be workable to those least conceivable. List the pros and cons of the solutions.

4. *Reach a tentative decision.* Decide which solution appears to be the best solution. Be prepared to stick to the proposed solution.

5. *Decide how to evaluate a solution once it is implemented.* Determine what criteria you will use to judge its effectiveness.

6. *Implement the solution.* Present the solution to those concerned. Inform them of the solution you have reached and, if necessary, give them instructions on how to implement the solution.

7. *Evaluate the results.* Make sure you monitor the results of the solution. Make sure that it is working as planned.

Conflict Resolution

The final supervisory challenge that we will look at is conflict resolution. Conflict can and does occur in the workplace between employees. As a supervisor, you cannot allow the conflict to escalate. If the conflict is not settled quickly by the supervisor, morale will suffer and so will job productivity. Conflict resolution can be handled through the "confronting/counseling" steps or by the "problem-solving method."

Another manner to handle conflict resolution is suggested by Joseph Berk and Susan Berk (1991) and is outlined:

1. *Determine if the conflict is personal or substantive.* A personal conflict is based largely on negative feelings between two or more people. A substantive conflict is based primarily over factual issues, and is not between two people. It is a conflict of an employee concerning a job-related issue.

2. *For both types of conflicts, call the employees to your office.* For issues of substantive conflicts, check the agency or organization's policies and procedures. See if they provide useful guidance. If not, check the issue

out with your supervisor or ask the legal counsel of your organization for an opinion. A substantive conflict may require the drafting of a new, or clearer, policy or procedure. It may require clarification of a union contract. If it reaches a point where the issue can be resolved, generally, a conflict of this magnitude should be brought to the attention of the first-line supervisor's boss. It is not showing weakness or incompetence to bring this type of issue to your supervisor.

3. *In personal conflicts, have the conflicting employees state their side of the problem.*

4. *Then, in personal conflicts, if the conflicting employees are unwilling to solve their differences, take appropriate action.* This could include: taking disciplinary action, reassigning one or both of the employees, or having another supervisor act as a go-between to monitor them (Berk, 1991).

The main thing about conflict resolution is to make sure that you, as the supervisor, acknowledge the conflict and take the appropriate action. Failure to do so could cause the conflict to continue and involve other employees. Furthermore, refusing to engage in conflict resolution conveys the message to employees that you are not concerned about their problems.

The supervisory challenges listed in this chapter and the methods on how to handle them should prepare the supervisors for the challenges they will encounter. Remember, these challenges will not go away, nor will they take care of themselves. Each challenge must be dealt with immediately and effectively by you—the supervisor. Failure to do so will cause the problem to escalate and involve other employees. Once this happens, supervisors will lose control of their assigned employees and lose their effectiveness as supervisors.

4 HOW TO ADMINISTER DISCIPLINE

One of the tasks that supervisors dread the most is administering discipline. Supervisors do not like to administer discipline for several reasons. Some do not like to administer discipline because they do not want to upset people. They do not want to be viewed unfavorably by the other employees; they do not want to be held liable for disciplinary action, and the list continues.

The unfortunate aspect of supervisors' jobs is the fact that they will have to administer discipline sooner or later. Granted, most people like to help others and do not want bad things to happen to those they know, and administering discipline appears to go against that philosophy of helping others. However, administering discipline is a necessity in the workforce.

Just like there are laws in society that we must obey or face the consequences, there are rules at work that we must obey or face the consequences. One aspect of the supervisory role is to ensure that the rules are followed. When they are not, we must take appropriate action.

Once a supervisor knows how and when to administer discipline, the fear of actually administering discipline is greatly diminished. This does not mean that the supervisor will enjoy administering discipline. It does mean that sooner or later, the supervisor will acknowledge the importance of administering discipline.

Imagine a work environment with no rules. Employees could do what they wanted when they wanted, and they could come to work and leave when they desired. There would be total chaos, and few people, if any, would tolerate it. Now, imagine a workplace with policies and procedures, but with a supervisor who is reluctant to enforce them. Several employees would follow the established policies and procedures, but many would not. There would be no incentive to go by the rules and conversely, no fear of discipline for not following the rules.

Next, imagine a work environment with established policies and procedures and a supervisor who not only follows the rules, but enforces the rules fairly and uniformly and administers discipline fairly, when warranted. For which type of the three work environments would you like to work? More than likely, you would choose the last example: a work environment with policies and procedures and a supervisor who enforces the rules and administers discipline, when warranted. Since you, as a supervisor, would choose the last example of a place where you would like to work, be assured that your employees would prefer to work in this type of environment, too.

Discipline is necessary to ensure compliance with the established policies and procedures. The purpose of discipline is to correct, not punish, people. When you view discipline with this philosophy, it is easier to accept the responsibility for administering discipline.

In some agencies, the frontline supervisors are not authorized to administer discipline. They, however, are authorized and expected to make a recommendation concerning discipline. Oftentimes, even though frontline supervisors only recommend disciplinary action, they are responsible for informing the employee of the discipline that is being imposed. Therefore, the employee still will view frontline supervisors as the ones who are administering the discipline, even though the frontline supervisors are just carrying out the directives from their supervisors.

Basic Steps in Discipline

Regardless of whether you are the one who administers the discipline, in other words, whether you can make a decision concerning discipline with no approval from your supervisor, or whether you can make a recommendation concerning the discipline to be imposed, there are some basic steps that should be followed. They include the following:

1. *Conduct an investigation concerning the alleged violation.* Gather all of the facts that you can to support or deny the policy violation allegation. During the investigation, it may be possible to determine that the employee did not commit the policy violation at issue. It also may be possible to discover that the employee committed other policy violations, or that other employees are involved.

2. *Once you have the facts, let the employees tell you their side of the story.* If they admit to the violation, it makes your job a lot easier.

3. *Decide whether the employees are in violation of the policy.* If they deny the allegations, you still need to determine whether, in fact, they are in violation of the policy.

4. *If you determine the employees are not in violation, the process is over.* However, you probably will want to inform the employees what could have happened if, in fact, they were found to be in violation. If you determine that the employees are in violation, proceed to step five.

5. *Determine what disciplinary action will be taken.* The disciplinary action must be proportionate to the policy violation committed. You also will want to take into consideration the employees' past work records and disciplinary records. If they are exemplary employees with no previous discipline, this could cause you to make a less severe recommendation. If they are employees with below-average work records who have a history of discipline problems, this could cause you to make more severe recommendations for discipline. You also will need to consider how other similar policy violations have been handled in the past.

6. *Impose the disciplinary action.* You personally should inform the employees what disciplinary action is going to be imposed. The disciplinary action to be imposed should be told verbally to the employees, and it should be stated in writing. The employees should sign an acknowledgment form indicating that they have been informed of the disciplinary action to be imposed. The acknowledgment also should include a statement that their signature only acknowledges receipt of the disciplinary action and does not indicate agreement with the disciplinary action.

7. *Inform employees of their right to grieve or appeal the disciplinary action, if they are eligible to grieve or appeal the decision.* As a general rule, employees on probationary status are not authorized to appeal any disciplinary action.

8. *Document the disciplinary meeting.* Make notes concerning what the employees said, did, and their attitudes. Keep this document separate from the disciplinary form that the employees signed. This documentation is for your records in case the employees file grievances or lawsuits.

9. *Make sure that the written notice of disciplinary action and the employee's signature on the acknowledgment form are placed in the employee's personnel file.* Keep a separate copy for your file. Give the employee a copy of the disciplinary letter and the signed acknowledgment form.

10. *Monitor employees after the discipline has been imposed.* The reason for monitoring employees is twofold: First, if the employees continue to commit the same, or other policy violations, you will need to take the appropriate action. Secondly, if the employees appear to be "distant" (which is common after a disciplinary action), you will need to counsel them and inform them that you expect them to perform their job to the best of their abilities and to use the past disciplinary action as a learning tool. You do not want a good or salvageable employee to go bad after disciplinary action has been imposed. Emphasize to them that the purpose of disciplinary action is to correct, not punish, the employee.

Other Factors in Administering Discipline

The following list contains other factors to consider when you are going to administer discipline:

1. *Conduct yourself in a professional manner.* Do not, under any circumstance, use profanity or derogatory language toward the employees you are disciplining. The employees may become upset and begin to act unprofessionally, but as the supervisor, you are expected to remain under control. If the employees do get upset, you will need to ask them to calm down. People act irrationally when they are upset, and you do not want to compound the disciplinary action.

2. *Do not make light of the policy violation or the disciplinary action that is going to be imposed.* For example, do not say something like, "This violation is not that big a deal and the discipline is not that bad," or worse yet, "My supervisor said I have to administer this discipline. This is his doing, not mine." Statements such as these send mixed messages to employees, such as: If the violation is no big deal, why am I being disciplined? Or, since a supervisor is imposing the discipline and it does not sound like my supervisor agrees with this action, I'll have my supervisor as a witness for me when I appeal this. Remember, discipline is a "big deal."

3. *Just as you are making notes to reflect what the employees said, their attitude, and so forth, the employees are making mental notes to write down later concerning what you said and your attitude.*

4. *There is no right against self-incrimination concerning a policy violation.* If the employees refuse to answer questions concerning a policy violation, impose the discipline as if you found them to be in violation. Additionally, some agencies terminate employees' employment if they refuse to answer questions concerning their involvement in a policy violation.

5. *Do not discuss specific disciplinary action with the line staff.* Only discuss the disciplinary action with other supervisors who have a legitimate need to know. Other employees should not know about the discipline that was imposed unless the disciplined employee tells them. Nothing is worse than a supervisor who administers discipline and then tells others about the discipline. Disciplinary action is personal and confidential. Treat it as such.

Enforcing the Rules and Regulations

Since enforcing the agency's or company's rules and regulations is a part of all supervisory and managerial jobs, and sooner or later most supervisors and managers must enforce established rules and regulations, be prepared to handle the discipline properly, and do so in accordance with the agency's established policies and procedures.

Management has the responsibility and at least a shared right to establish the rules and regulations necessary to ensure the attainment of the agency's goals and mission, and to protect the welfare of the agency's members. Most employees want control and discipline, orderly conduct, and compliance with work rules, especially from their coworkers. In fact, another purpose of discipline is to ensure agency goals are carried out and to protect the welfare of agency members (American Correctional Association, 1991b).

Progressive Discipline

Discipline should be progressive in nature. Typical progressive disciplinary steps, which are a part of most policy and procedures manuals, include the following:

1. *Oral warning.* This consists of the supervisor telling the employee what is wrong and what is to be corrected. It is important to keep a written record of the oral warning.

2. *Written warning.* A written warning generally is issued after an oral warning. In the written warning, the supervisor specifically should state the policy that was violated, what corrective action needs to be taken, a time frame in which to correct the inappropriate behavior, and a warning about what the next disciplinary step will be if the inappropriate behavior is not corrected, as specified.

3. *Suspension.* This occurs when the employee receives time off from work without pay, usually after an oral and/or a written warning.

4. *Termination.* This is the last step. It usually is taken after the previous disciplinary measures have been implemented.

Progressive discipline is a multistep process of repeated warnings, coupled with opportunities for employees to correct unacceptable behavior. Each step of the progressive discipline must be documented.

Some agencies have the progressive disciplinary process clearly outlined. Agencies with this type of progressive discipline system have a disciplinary manual with a list of violations and the action that is to be taken for each offense. For example, an offense such as "tardiness in reporting to work," generally is handled as follows:

First offense: Oral warning

Second offense: Written warning

Third offense: One-day suspension

Fourth offense: Three-day suspension

Fifth offense: Termination from employment

Other offenses are more serious and start off with a one-day suspension, then a three-day suspension, followed by termination from employment. Other offenses are listed in the employee handbook as a "penalty to be determined by circumstances." This leaves it up to the supervisor to make an appropriate recommendation concerning the discipline to be imposed. Finally, there are offenses which are so serious that termination from employment is the only appropriate response without the use of the normal progressive disciplinary steps. An example of this type of offense would be an assault on a supervisor.

When an agency has a clearly outlined disciplinary process, it is easier for the supervisor to make a recommendation concerning discipline because the discipline for the offense already is mandated by policy. However, the supervisor still will need to follow the disciplinary action steps outlined earlier. When the disciplinary process is clearly outlined, it is advisable to follow it. Following a clearly outlined disciplinary process negates the likelihood of employees successfully using a defense of "unfair treatment" by their supervisor on an appeal or in a grievance.

Agencies that use such a standardized progressive disciplinary process normally have a time frame attached to the violation concerning the action to be taken. For example, most violations are kept in an employee's personnel file for a period of twelve- to-eighteen months. Normally, oral and written warnings are kept for twelve months and suspensions for eighteen months. During this time, the violations can be combined and the discipline increased.

For example, if an employee is late for work, the first offense requires an oral warning. Then, the same employee one month later commits a violation that requires an oral warning. The supervisor could go to the next step, written warning, because the employee already has received an oral warning, albeit an oral warning for another offense. Supervisors should use caution when deviating from the established disciplinary process and be prepared to defend their actions, even though under some circumstances such action may be warranted.

There are several benefits of a progressive disciplinary system. The first benefit is that employees are given notice of the conduct that will not be tolerated and the consequences that might occur as a result of the continued poor performance or inappropriate behavior. They also are given the opportunity to correct their unacceptable job performance.

Another benefit is that if the progressive disciplinary system is implemented and used properly, the employer will be able to demonstrate that employees were told about a problem in writing, and were given adequate opportunities to correct their substandard job performance. Finally, proper use of a progressive disciplinary system gives the employer a written record that will be beneficial in heading off or defending lawsuits that result from the disciplinary actions that were imposed.

However, the progressive disciplinary system has some problems, too. Progressive discipline, if not used consistently and uniformly, actually will work against the employer and for the employee. Progressive discipline is time consuming and requires a lot of work from the supervisor. It takes time for the supervisor to counsel the employee, retrain the employee, and document all of the actions that the supervisor took to help the employee.

Regardless of some of the apparent disadvantages of a progressive disciplinary system, the consistent and uniformed application of a progressive discipline system will help produce better work output from employees and, at the same time, negate or greatly reduce the likelihood of employee claims of unfair treatment and lawsuits.

Listed next is suggested language that should be included in the disciplinary documentation, as indicated:

Oral Warning

Sample

> On (date), I gave (employee's name) an oral warning for (list the violation). He/she said (state what the employee said in regards to the oral warning). I explained the rule to him/her regarding (state the rule violated and state that you explained this to the employee). I also warned the employee about future violations of this kind, and that any rules' violation will result in discipline. The employee is aware that a copy of this oral warning will be placed in his/her file.
>
> (Your signed name).

Written Warning

In a written warning, be sure that the following points are covered: the purpose of the warning, the identified problem, the policy that was violated, the corrective action that is to be taken, a time frame in which to complete the corrective action, and the consequences of future or continued violations.

Sample

> On (date), you (state the action the employees did). This is in violation of (state the policy number and quote the policy statement). On (date) you received an oral warning for (state the offense). This letter will serve as a written reprimand for violation of (state the policy number). Be advised that effective immediately, you are expected to (state what the employees are expected to do to come into compliance with the policy they violated). You are hereby put on notice that any violations of this policy or any other policy will result in further disciplinary action, which could include suspension without pay or termination from employment.
>
> (Your signed name)
> (Title)
> (Employee's signature)

Suspension from Employment

The notice of the suspension without pay should be in writing. The following format can be used.

Sample Suspension Notice

Effective (date), you are hereby suspended without pay for (state the length of the suspension). The length of the suspension will be from (state start date) until (state end date). You are to return to work on (state date). The reason for this suspension is (state the reason why the employee is being suspended).

(Your signed name)
(Title)
(Employee's signature)

Termination from Employment

The following format can be used as a guide for developing a termination letter.

Sample Termination Letter

Effective (date) you are hereby discharged from employment. The reason for this personnel action is (state the reason why the individual is being fired). You are to turn in all of your department-issued property immediately to (state the person's name).

(Your signed name)
(Your title)
(Employee's signature)

Obviously, the suggested formats listed can be used as guidelines and will need to be modified to fit each situation. You may wish to get guidance from the legal counsel of your agency or firm on the proper wording of these materials. One thing you do not want to do is to issue written documentation to the employee that is too lengthy. Succinctly state the reasons for the adverse personnel action and stick to the facts. Do not elaborate on each point in the disciplinary letter.

Make sure that you only list the policy violations in the disciplinary letter that you can prove. Do not list violations that cannot be substantiated.

Due Process

By following these suggested formats, you will ensure that employees have received due process. Due process basically means making sure that employees are afforded their rights and are treated fairly.

In each of the disciplinary letters (oral warning, written warning, suspension, and termination) the employees must sign their name to the letter acknowledging receipt of it. If they refuse to sign their name, have another supervisor witness the refusal. If the employee refuses to sign an acknowledgment of receipt, include the following statement in the disciplinary letter:

> On (date), (employee's name) refused to sign his/her name to this letter acknowledging receipt of this letter. A copy of this letter was personally given to (employee's name) by (your name). (Employee's name) refusal to sign this letter and his/her receipt of this letter was witnessed by (witness' name). You and the witness will need to sign your names to the form and date it.

Employees need to be given a chance to sign their name to any personnel action, to acknowledge receipt, or given the opportunity to refuse to sign their name. Regardless, if they sign their name or not, the employee must be given a copy of it. Additionally, if the employee is eligible to appeal or grieve the disciplinary action, you will need to include the following statement in each of the disciplinary letters: "You have the right to appeal the reasonableness of this personnel action by using the established grievance procedure."

Inform employees being disciplined of the grievance procedure to ensure that their due process is not violated. It is much better to have employees use the grievance procedure than to file a lawsuit against you and your organization because you neglected to tell them of their right to appeal a disciplinary action.

Termination

Initiating discipline against an employee is a serious task and should not be taken lightly. This is especially true if the disciplinary action to be imposed is termination from employment. Before you terminate employees from employment, or make the recommendation for such termination, consider the following: how long the employees have been employed, their overall job performance, the record of their past disciplinary actions, how past disciplinary actions have been handled, whether the documentation supports the decision to terminate the employees, and if there is any other action that you could take instead of termination.

Ask yourself these questions to make sure that termination from employment is not only the appropriate action, but the only alternative. Moreover, these are questions that the grievance board and/or judge and jury will want answered to uphold a decision of termination from employment.

As you can see, disciplining an employee, or making a recommendation for discipline, is not an easy task. It is a task that supervisors dread and sometimes fear. It requires a lot of work.

Remember that subordinate personnel will judge you by the way in which you handle the discipline of your staff. The key is to be fair and consistent. Also, make sure that you keep accurate written documentation on each disciplinary action.

Although discipline is not a pleasurable task, it is a necessary one. Supervisors who know how and when to administer discipline will discover that to have an efficient running shift, discipline is a necessity. Furthermore, it is not the supervisor who is disciplining staff members, it is the staff members, by their own actions, who are bringing the discipline on themselves.

Exit Interview

One final subject in regards to disciplinary action is the exit interview. No matter if employees resign in lieu of termination, are, in fact, terminated, or resign in good standing, they should be given an exit interview. An exit interview allows employees an opportunity to give the reasons that they are leaving their job, to state what they liked and did not like about the job. They should be given a chance to "rate" their supervisor because useful information can be obtained from outgoing employees. They might be able to give you information that can be used to make positive changes in the work environment. Their candid response can make you aware of problems on the job, and it can give you a chance to take corrective action, if necessary.

The exit interview gives the employees a last chance to air any grievances that they might have with the department, and it will help ward off potential lawsuits. The exit interview should employ a written form that the employees can fill out and turn in prior to their departure. The employee also should be given a chance to meet with a supervisor in person to discuss the exit interview. The exit interview is uncomfortable at first, but once you get used to it, you will find it to be beneficial.

5 HOW TO RESPOND TO GRIEVANCES

Another aspect of the supervisor's job that is almost as dreaded as administering discipline is that of handling grievances. Handling grievances can be stressful for a supervisor. A grievance almost always puts the supervisor on the defensive because, normally, the grievance is a result of the supervisor's actions. In this chapter, we examine ways to respond to grievances and help make this process less stressful.

A *grievance* is a complaint filed by an employee. The grievance can be about discipline, working conditions, or it may allege that one or more policies have been misapplied.

The best way to combat grievances is to prevent them from occurring in the first place. The supervisor may prevent many grievances by the use of good supervisory skills. Additionally, consistently following the policies and fairly administering discipline within the established guidelines also helps in reducing the number of grievances that employees file.

All grievances should be in writing so that there is a written record concerning the alleged complaint. Likewise, all responses to the grievances should be in writing, too. At times, this is written out in policy and procedure manuals or in union contracts. Ideally, there should be a standardized form for grievances that should contain the following information:

1. Date the grievance was filed

2. Name of employee who filed the grievance

3. A statement of the reason the grievance is being filed

4. The policy that allegedly was violated

5. Steps the employee took to prevent filing the grievance

6. The desired outcome or what the employee hopes to accomplish by filing the grievance

7. The supervisor's written response to the grievance

Once supervisors receive the written grievance, they need to schedule a meeting with the employee to discuss the grievance. The purpose of this meeting is to find out as much information about the grievance as you can. Make sure that you listen to the employee's side of the complaint. The employee needs to tell you about the policy that allegedly was violated.

You need this information so that you can begin an investigation into this matter. You will need to know how similar grievances have been handled in the past. Remember, once you reach a decision, your decision sets a precedent on how future similar grievances will be handled.

Finally, once you have completed the investigation and reached your decision, inform all who are involved in the grievance of the outcome of it. This notification should be in writing, and a written record should be kept for future reference.

Features of Grievance Procedures

Grievance procedures exist in most workplaces and usually contain the same important features:

1. The procedure usually defines a grievance as a claim by an employee or the union that the employer violated the contract. If the union is involved, this means that the union is the moving party that pushes the grievance through the procedure.

2. Grievances must be expressed in writing and managerial responses usually are given in writing (often after an oral first step).

3. The procedure guarantees employees the right to be represented by the union, which means the grievants will have an advocate to press their

claim upon management, and there usually are various procedural rules that protect the union's advocacy role.

4. The procedure specifies several steps (usually about four) through which the unresolved grievance moves as it is appealed to higher levels within the organization and union.

5. There are explicit time limits for filing grievances and for appealing them to the next higher step.

6. The prearbitration resolution of a grievance requires mutual agreement between the union and the employer. This gives the union a strong voice in prearbitration grievance resolution.

7. The terminal grievance procedure step almost always is arbitration. Arbitration is a hearing which results in a binding decision by an external arbitrator who is selected and compensated jointly by the union and the employer, which also gives the union a strong voice in the arbitrated resolution of grievances (Ferris et al., 1995).

While this procedure pertains to grievances filed in a unionized workplace, it is similar to the grievance procedure in a nonunion workplace. Examples of the normal steps taken in a nonunion workplace to resolve a grievance include the following:

1. The employee will put the grievance in writing within seven days of the date in which the basis for the grievance occurred or was made known to the employee. Then, the employee will forward the written grievance to his or her supervisor.

2. The supervisor will review the written grievance and meet with the grievant within seven days of the receipt of the grievance.

3. After listening to the employee and other witnesses, and reviewing pertinent documentation relevant to the grievance, the supervisor will inform the employee of his or her decision. The decision should be made within seven days from the meeting with the employee. The decision or the supervisor's response should be in writing.

4. Upon receipt of the supervisor's decision, the employee may take the grievance to the next step if the employee is not satisfied with the decision from the supervisor. Normally, the employee must go to the next step within seven days from receipt of the supervisor's decision. If the

employee is satisfied with the decision from the supervisor, the grievance process is finished.

5. Once the grievance is forwarded to the next level, the grievance board (or it may be the top administrator) will set a meeting date with the employee and all witnesses (which usually includes the supervisor who heard the grievance at the first step). The meeting normally takes place within fourteen days from the receipt of the grievance by the grievance board.

6. At the grievance hearing, the grievants once again will state the reasons for the appeal and the desired remedy. The employee also may present witnesses. Once grievants have presented their side of the grievance, the supervisor who heard the grievance initially will present facts concerning why the decision should be upheld. The grievance board has the right to question all parties concerned and call other relevant witnesses to help make a fair and just decision.

7. The grievance board will put their decision in writing and inform the grievant and the supervisor of their decision. Normally, the parties are informed of the decision within fourteen days from the date of the hearing. The grievance board can take the following action on a grievance:

   • Uphold the supervisor's decision

   • Uphold the supervisor's decision with modifications, in other words, make the discipline less severe, work out a compromise if it is a nondisciplinary grievance, and so forth

   • Find in favor of the grievant, in other words, overrule the supervisor's decision (the grievance board cannot increase the discipline or make the supervisor's decision more strict)

8. Once the employees are in receipt of the grievance board's decision, the grievance process is at an end. However, the employees could file a lawsuit in federal court against the employer if they felt the decision was unfair and discriminated against them, and they then could pursue the grievance through the court system.

Encourage the Grievance Process

Of course, employees should not be discouraged from using the grievance process if they are entitled to use it. In fact, if employees threaten to use the grievance process against you, they should be encouraged to do so. This shows the employee that you are confident of your decision and welcome a review of your decision by a fair and impartial third party. If employees threaten to use the grievance process against you, and you do not encourage them to do so, this will tell the employees that you are not sure of your decision and do not want a third party to review it. Furthermore, if you discourage employees' use of the grievance process, you could be violating their right to due process.

As a supervisor, you will make decisions that are not popular and employees will disagree. This is particularly true when the decision pertains to discipline. Therefore, make sure that you follow the rules, are fair with all employees, and can back up all of your decisions. Once employees are convinced that you treat all employees fairly and do not play favorites, they will file few grievances.

6 HOW TO CONDUCT EMPLOYEE PERFORMANCE EVALUATIONS

Another aspect of the supervisor's role that can be as stressful as administering discipline or responding to grievances, is that of conducting an employee performance evaluation. In this chapter, we will examine various steps to prepare you for conducting the evaluation and discuss mistakes to avoid in preparing the written evaluation.

Importance of Employee Performance Evaluations

Conducting proper employee performance evaluations is one of the more important tasks that you, as a supervisor, will do. Your evaluation of employees' job performances could determine if the employees will get promoted, be given a pay raise, or have the opportunity to transfer to a job with more responsibility. It also could determine if the employees will get no pay raise or perhaps be terminated from employment. For these reasons, it is important that you treat performance evaluations as though the employees' jobs depend upon what you say, or do not say, in the evaluation.

Supervisors dread performance evaluations because to do them properly takes time and a lot of work. Also, most people feel uncomfortable rating another person. However, supervisors owe it to their employees to rate their job performance fairly, even if this means giving them a justifiable low rating. Employees have a right to know if their job performance is below standard, so that they can take action to bring their job performance to an acceptable standard.

A performance appraisal is the process of evaluating the performance and qualifications of employees. This is done in terms of the requirements of the job for which they are employed, for purposes of administration, including placement, for selection for promotion, for provision of financial rewards, and for other actions (Heyel, 1973).

Through a systematic rating procedure, management maintains a record of the relative worth of its personnel and thereby is able to make sound decisions regarding employment, placement, transfers, promotions, dismissals, and individual salary rewards related to worth. Despite their imperfections, appraisal records are relatively objective and provide information that often cannot be obtained in any other way (Heyel, 1973).

Since performance appraisal data is used to make many important personnel decisions, such as promotions, pay raises, and terminations, it is important that the appraisal be done properly. Failure to conduct a performance appraisal properly could lead to grievances and perhaps lawsuits. This, of course, can be avoided if you make sure that your evaluation is of the employees' job performance, not personality and other nonjob-related matters.

Fair Performance Appraisals

The following recommendations should assist employers in conducting fair performance appraisal.

Use Legally Defensible Appraisal Procedures

Personnel decisions should be based on a formal, standardized-performance appraisal system. Performance appraisal processes should be uniform for all employees within a job group, and decisions based on those performance appraisals should be monitored for differences according to race, sex, national origin, religion, disability, or age of employees.

Specific performance standards should be formally communicated to all employees. Employees should be able to formally review the appraisal results. There should be a formal appeal process for employees to rebut judgments of the rater. Raters should be provided with written instructions and training on how to conduct systematic, unbiased appraisals.

Use Legally Defensible Appraisal Content

Performance-appraisal content should be based on a job analysis. Appraisals based on employee traits should be avoided. Objective, verifiable performance data (such as output, errors, and other measurable/countable results) should be used, whenever possible. Specific job-related performance functions, dimensions, standards, and goals or objectives should be used rather than global measures or a single overall assessment of performance. Performance dimensions or objectives should be assigned weights to reflect their relative importance in calculating a composite performance score.

Use Legally Defensible Documentation of Appraisal Results

A thorough written record of evidence leading to termination decisions should be maintained and may include performance appraisals and notes on performance counseling. These would be used to advise employees of performance deficits and to assist poor performers to make needed improvements. Written documentation for extreme ratings should be required. This may include specific examples of behavior, results, or work products. Documentation requirements should be consistent among raters.

Employ Legally Defensible Raters

Raters should be trained in how to use the appraisal system. Raters must have the opportunity to observe the employee firsthand or to review important ratee performance products. Use of more than one rater is desirable to lessen the amount of influence of any one rater and to reduce the effects of biases (Ferris et al, 1995).

Revision of Performance Appraisal System

Once a well-designed performance appraisal system has been implemented, the work still is not done. An appraisal system has to be reviewed and revised, as needed, on a continuing basis. Be sure that the performance evaluation rates the employee on identifiable, articulated, measurable outcomes. Ask yourself: Does this evaluation give us a fair, overall picture of this employee's job performance? If it does not, you will want to make appropriate changes. If it does, you still will need to monitor the performance evaluation system to make sure that it keeps up with the job description of the employee(s) you are rating.

Guidelines for Effective Performance Appraisals

Preparing for an effective performance appraisal actually begins when the previous appraisal ends. To assist the supervisor in preparing to conduct a performance appraisal interview, the following steps can be used as a guideline:

1. *Keep accurate documentation throughout the evaluation period.* Do not wait until the week before the appraisal is due and attempt to recall how the employee's job performance has been during this performance-evaluation cycle. Use of a daily log may be helpful. In your log, note how each employee performed on a given day, any problems, any commendations, shift assignments, and so forth. Your log is your recordbook. Use it to your advantage.

2. *Communicate the performance standards to all employees when they are initially hired and throughout the performance appraisal period.* Employees need to know what they are expected to do and what is an acceptable level of job performance. If they do not know what is expected of them, they will do what they think is right.

3. *The performance appraisal should contain no surprises.* This means that employees should not be told on their evaluation that they have been doing a particular job task incorrectly for the entire rating period. If they were doing it wrong, they should have been told when it was first noticed, not a year later on their performance appraisal. However, if they were told and did not correct the behavior, that, of course, should be on their performance appraisal.

4. *Focus on employees' strengths.* Too often, performance evaluations focus on employees' weaknesses. Let them know what they do well.

5. *Set realistic goals for improvement.* Not only should you state the employees' strengths, you also need to make them aware of any substandard job performance that needs improvement. If you identify areas that need improvement, you need to set forth a step-by-step procedure concerning how they can improve for the next performance evaluation period. Also, the goals you set for improvement must be realistic, attainable, and within the employee's capabilities.

6. *Rate the employee fairly.* Too often, supervisors will rate employees too high, or right in the middle because it is easier to do it that way, and normally no one will complain. If you do this, you are doing the employee, yourself, and your agency a grave disservice. Sometimes, the truth hurts, such as telling employees that they need to improve, but employees have the right to be rated fairly and objectively. Rate employees against established job performance standards and not other employees. If you rate them against clearly objective standards, they cannot accuse you of playing favorites and rating them low because you allegedly do not like them.

7. *Give yourself plenty of time to make a fair performance appraisal.* You cannot or should not be able to write a performance evaluation in a few minutes. Since you are evaluating employees for a whole year's worth of employment, you owe it to them to give them a fair, accurate, honest performance appraisal. Also, make sure that your appraisal of the employees covers the entire rating period and not just the most recent few weeks.

Preparing For Performance Appraisal Interviews

Once all of the steps are accomplished, you will be ready to conduct the actual performance appraisal interview. The performance appraisal interview occurs when you actually sit down and discuss the employees' performance appraisals with them. Never give employees their performance appraisal without discussing it with them and giving them time to ask questions. Allow adequate time for the actual performance appraisal interview and make sure the interview is conducted in private.

Preparation for the performance appraisal is a lengthy process that entails several steps. Performance management is not a single event. It continues throughout the appraisal period and when the appraisal period is over, performance management does not come to an end; it continues. Therefore, the eight-step process, presented next, forms a circle. Step eight of this year's appraisal period happens at the same meeting as step one of the next year's appraisal. According to Swan (1991), this eight-step performance appraisal consists of the following steps:

1. *A performance plan and development plan are agreed to by the supervisor and the employee.* The supervisor sets performance objectives and outlines a performance plan with the employee in the appraisal discussion. A development plan is agreed to, and the standards of performance for the performance factors are clarified.

2. *The employee receives feedback, coaching, and counseling.* Documentation is maintained for the next year. Throughout the following year, the supervisor conducts periodic informal or formal feedback sessions. The supervisor documents incidents relevant to the employees' performance, and lets the employees know how they are progressing on the goals set and how they are performing with respect to the agreed-on standards. If necessary, the supervisor intervenes to improve performance or to offer coaching and counseling.

3. *As the time of the appraisal approaches and prior to writing of the performance appraisal, the supervisor solicits the employees' self-evaluation.* The intent of this is to prepare the employees for the appraisal discussion and to provide the supervisor with an additional source of input when writing the appraisal. Such self-evaluation does not mean that employees are being asked to write their own appraisals.

4. *The supervisor meets with the employee to discuss the employee's self-evaluation.* Still, prior to writing the appraisal, the supervisor and the employee meet to review the employee's self-evaluation. The primary goal of this meeting is to get information from the employee. This input may be used as an aid in writing the appraisal and preparing for the appraisal discussion.

5. *Supervisors complete their portion of the performance appraisal by using all of the sources of information available.* This includes the performance data gathered throughout the review period, the employee's input, and feedback from internal and external sources, when appropriate.

6. *Supervisors preview the appraisal with their supervisor or human resources representative.* In some agencies, this step is required. If it is not required, it still is a good idea to do this. Your supervisor is one-step removed from the interaction and can bring a fresh perspective to it. You know what you meant when you wrote it. Yet, it may not be apparent to you that what you wrote has another interpretation. Having someone else review it before you present it to the employee may help catch that interpretation and prevent misunderstandings, embarrassment, or an argument. Then, too, a manager one level up may be in a better position than you to make sure that your procedures are in line with the organization's policy. Finally, your manager or a representative from the personnel department can check the legal ramifications of the appraisal.

7. *The supervisor schedules the appraisal meeting with the employee.* The supervisor sets the date, time, and location for the meeting that will give both parties an opportunity to focus on the appraisal without interruption. Budget enough time for the entire appraisal and development discussion.

8. *The supervisor conducts the appraisal discussion.* The supervisor discusses the completed appraisal and development plan with the employee. The supervisor should maintain control but give ample opportunity for discussion. The supervisor should give the employee an opportunity to write comments into the record if the employee wishes to do so. The employee's signature affirms only his or her participation in the process. It affirms that the performance appraisal has taken place, not necessarily that the employee agrees with its content. During this same meeting, you will work out the performance plan for next year (Swan, 1991, pp. 47-51).

These steps will give the supervisor a solid foundation on which to build to prepare for the appraisal interview. Next, we will examine how to avoid some common errors to ensure a successful, productive performance appraisal interview.

While there is not a single script that you can develop to ensure a perfect performance appraisal interview, prepare yourself for the interview. Failure to prepare for the interview is a reason these types of interviews do not always go as planned. You will need to establish rapport and listen attentively when employees speak about their job performance. Withhold judgment about employees until they have had an opportunity to explain their poor job performance. Try to remain objective throughout the interview process. Keep in mind that receiving a performance evaluation can be stressful for the employees, so approach the interview in a professional, objective manner.

Conducting Performance Appraisals

Apart from the strengths and weaknesses inherent in the nature of a given performance appraisal system, there are errors of implementation that can be made no matter what techniques you use. In fact, the way your performance appraisal system is administered and the training given to the managers using it probably has more to do with the effectiveness of the appraisal than any other factor. Some performance appraisal systems prevent or reduce these errors more than others, but all are subject to some of them.

The six most common appraisal errors in conducting performance appraisals include the following:

1. Inadequately defining standards of performance

2. Relying on gut feelings

3. Insufficient or unclear documenting of performance

4. Not allotting adequate time for the discussion

5. Too much talking by the supervisor

6. Not having a follow-up plan (Swan, 1991)

Of course, the employee may miscomprehend performance standards. In this case, it is up to the supervisor to explain them so that the employee understands what is expected of him or her.

Writing the Performance Appraisal

Because writing the performance appraisal properly is just as important as conducting a proper appraisal interview, we will look at the actual writing of the appraisal. This section describes how to write the performance appraisal and what errors to avoid.

In writing the performance appraisal, be fair and objective. Appraisals in and of themselves are subjective, so how can you remain objective? One way is to avoid the common errors. Industrial psychologists have categorized the most common rating errors. They including the following:

1. *Similar to me.* This is a tendency to rate people higher if they are similar to you, or rating them lower if they are different from you.

2. *Positive lenience.* This is rating persons higher than they deserve. Rating persons higher than they deserve is demotivating and fosters disrespect for the process, and you.

3. *Negative lenience.* This occurs when a supervisor is reluctant to assign high ratings to individuals, or the supervisor may rate people lower than they deserve.

4. *Halo/Horns effect.* This is being overly influenced by a single favorable trait or unfavorable trait. Alternatively, it may be allowing the previous supervisor's evaluation of the employee to unduly affect your evaluation of the same employee.

5. *Recency effect.* This means rating someone down or up based solely on recent events and ignoring the individual's performance during the entire rating period.

6. *Attribution bias.* This is a tendency to see poor performance more within the control of the individual and to see superior performance as more influenced by external factors.

7. *Stereotyping.* This is generalizing across a group and not recognizing individual differences.

8. *Contrast effect.* This is making comparisons by evaluating the employee relative to the person last evaluated.

9. *First impression.* This is forming an initial positive or negative judgment and then ignoring or distorting subsequent information to avoid changing the initial impression.

10. *Central tendency.* This is placing people in the middle of the scale or close to the midpoint to avoid extreme positions (Swan, 1991, pp 120-123).

A performance appraisal should be geared to employees' past behavior, covering the time since their last performance review to the present. Normally, a performance appraisal should be given annually with the exception of employees in a probationary status; these employees should be given reviews at intervals of three-and-six months, and annually thereafter (Patton, Jr., 1982). To be prepared for the appraisal interview, supervisors must make sure that they avoid the ten rating errors in writing the performance appraisal and the six conduct errors of supervisors during the performance appraisal.

Objectivity

There is no way to entirely eliminate the subjective element from judgments about employee performance. If supervisors have a mountain of facts at their disposal, their chances of being objective are greater than if they only have a few. But supervisors still have to interpret these facts and decide which facts are the most meaningful. Writing a fair, objective performance appraisal contains the following three steps:

1. Gathering and analyzing data throughout the appraisal period

2. Rating the performance based on this information

3. Writing the narrative portions of the appraisal (Swan, 1991, pp. 123)

When supervisors write the narrative portion of the performance appraisal, they must be sure that everything they put in writing is factual and can be proven. They should not make subjective statements such as, "It appears that you have trouble getting to work on time." Rather, they should make it a factual statement such as, "You were late to work on the following dates . . ."

Supervisors should state definitive goals. For example, do not say, "During the next six months, try to improve your attendance record." Rather, state, "During the next six months, you are expected to come to work on time as scheduled, unless excused by your supervisor in advance." Also, supervisors should be sure that their comments are both grammatically correct and spelled correctly. These steps make the report sound and look professional.

Supervisors should be careful of what they say to the employee in the course of the performance evaluation. Stick to job-related items only. They should not make any comments about the employee's job performance that cannot be verified. Also, they should not make a reference to employees' poor job performances being related to their age or sex. For example, do not say, "I'm sure the reason you cannot handle the inmates so well is because of your age (or because you are a female and are not as strong as the males on your shift)." A good rule of thumb for performance appraisal is this: Write each appraisal and conduct each appraisal interview as though you will wind up in court. State only the facts, and stick to what you can prove.

7 HOW TO HIRE QUALIFIED STAFF

As a first-line supervisor, you probably will not be responsible for placing advertisements in the newspaper for job openings, nor will you be responsible for hiring new employees. Yet, at some time, you probably will be asked to assist with the hiring process, perhaps by sitting on an interview panel. If you do sit on an interview panel, you may be responsible for making a recommendation for hiring an employee. To do this, you must conduct questioning that is appropriate and in accordance with applicable laws pertaining to the hiring procedure. For example, as a general rule, you cannot ask questions that bear no relevance to the job qualifications. Avoid questions that pertain to age, gender, religion, and disability.

Negligent Hiring

Believe it or not, you could be held liable for negligent hiring if you do not make the right decision! This statement is not intended to make supervisors reluctant to sit on an interview panel. It is intended to make supervisors cognizant of how important their recommendation for employment can be.

The employer and those making the hiring decision can be held liable for negligent hiring under the law, such as: if the employer should have known that the employee was unfit for employment but failed to take the necessary steps to determine the employee's fitness for the job, or if the employer knew the employee was unfit but hired the employee anyway, or when the employer discovers that the employee is unfit after hiring and the employer fails to take corrective action such as retraining, reassigning, or discharging the employee.

The Hiring Process

Generally speaking, the normal hiring process for a correctional setting is as follows:

1. An advertisement is placed in the local newspaper and/or professional magazines.

2. The personnel department reviews applications and forwards the application of those who are qualified to the department head.

3. The department head, or designee, reviews the applications of the qualified applicants and selects the applications of those who they plan to interview.

4. Prospective employees are contacted for interviews.

5. The administrator convenes an interview panel and the applicants are interviewed.

6. The interview panel submits a list of names to the administrator for hiring.

7. Selected applicants are given a conditional job offer and agree to a physical examination, drug screen, and background check.

8. The applicant is hired and begins the training.

This hiring process, from the time an advertisement is placed in the newspaper up until the applicants are hired, can take up to six weeks. The process is lengthy, but it is necessary to ensure that only the most qualified applicants are hired.

Preparing for the Interview

Once you are notified that you will be on an interview board, you will need to prepare for the interview process. Some agencies use standardized questions where the same questions are asked of each applicant, and some structure the questions based on the information in the applicant's resume.

Regardless of the structure of the questions to be asked during the interview, there are certain steps you should undertake to prepare for it. You should be familiar with the job description and know the qualifications that are required for the positions for which you will be interviewing candidates. You should review the applications and/or resumes of the applicants and only seek to interview those who meet the qualifications for the job. When conducting the job interview, only ask questions that are job related and ask the applicants the same questions. Finally, once the interviews are completed, check the references of the applicants to make sure that the applicant(s) were truthful on their application.

Developing a List of Questions

One of the steps in preparing for the interview is developing a list of pertinent questions. If your agency uses a standardized list of questions, you will want to review them. Perhaps the questions need to be revised from time to time. If they do, you will want to inform your supervisor of what you think the changes need to be. Examine all the questions asked to see if they elicit the information you need to make a sound hiring decision.

What makes a good interview question? According to Bell (1989), all good interview questions share the following attributes:

1. *Each question should have a purpose.* The interviewer designs questions to achieve certain ends—most often to elicit data for decision making. Whether broad or narrow in scope, each question should be aimed at a target of some kind. For example: "Are there any circumstances that will prevent you from working shift work?" is a valid question. However, "Do you have children who need a baby-sitter if you work shift work?" is not a good question. This second question has no valid work-related relevance. All you should be concerned about is whether a person can work shift work. This second question also is disproportionately discriminatory to females and to single parents.

2. *Each question should be tied to job requirements.* For both legal reasons and simple efficiency, interview questions should not stray into areas unrelated to the job. Interviewers, of course, can ask "getting to know you" questions, but even these should try to draw out personal characteristics and attitudes important to success in your organization. For example, "Corrections is a stressful line of work. How do you relieve your stress?" is a good question, but "A lot of us like to party after work. Do you drink?" is not a good question.

3. *Each question should be focused and clear.* Poor questions, in turn, produce confused, misdirected answers from interviewees. For example, "What aspect of corrections do you like best?" is a good question. Ask questions that are clear and to the point. Do not ask long, confusing, compound questions. Only ask one question at a time and give the interviewee time to answer that question.

4. *Each question must be repeatable.* Interview questions should be general enough so that they can be asked of each applicant. This allows you to compare candidates.

5. *Each question should have a meaningful place in the entire sequence of interview questions.* In successful interviews, questions follow a meaningful sequence (Bell, 1989, pp. 96-98). You may wish to write out all the questions you intend to ask, then structure them into a logical order.

Be sure that you have time to review all applications before each interview. Also, if the interview panel meets a few days before the interviews take place, suggest that the group decide what questions they will ask, who will ask what questions, what they are looking for in an applicant, and the order in which the applicants will be interviewed. In general, interviewers should ask open-ended questions, questions that require more than a "yes" or "no" answer.

Reasons for Bad Hiring Decisions

Regardless of how well an interview panel prepares itself, it still is possible to make a bad hiring decision. Bad hiring decisions usually are made because of one or more of the following reasons:

1. Poor analysis of the job functions

2. Poor analysis of the necessary personality and skill match

3. Inadequate initial screening

4. Inadequate interviewing or questioning techniques

5. Poor use of second opinions

6. Company and career/money expectations were over or inappropriately sold

7. References were not checked (Yate, 1987, p. 19)

Being Prepared

By being prepared for the interviewing process, you should be able to overcome the problems pertaining to making a bad hiring decision. The point of the interview process is to select applicants who are able to do the job based on their qualifications and background, who are willing to do the job based on their motivation and desire exhibited during the interview process, and who are manageable once they are selected.

Employee Word of Mouth

Another method of attracting qualified applicants is to ask your existing employees if they know of qualified people who would like to work for your organization. When employees are informed of job opportunities and encouraged to spread the word about them, the benefits of networking are infinite. To inform your employees requires an internal job posting system and to encourage their help requires an incentive referral program (Visconti and Brounstein, 1992, p. 39). However, be certain to also list your job in a major newspaper so there is no hint of any lack of affirmative action or equal opportunity.

Supervisors Should Make A Good Impression on Candidates

There are many qualified applicants looking for jobs. Once they respond to an advertisement and are interviewed, the supervisors play an integral role in helping the applicants decide whether they will take the job if it is offered to them. Supervisors should want to make a good impression on all applicants, because they are representatives of their agency. How the applicants view you will shape their overall opinion about the entire agency. Be sure that you are professional, businesslike, and friendly. Answer their questions honestly. Do not oversell your organization, but do paint a realistic picture of it. The applicants will appreciate your honesty during the interview. Your honesty will reverberate with the candidates if they are hired.

8 POLICY AND PROCEDURE

Throughout this book, we talked about enforcing policy and procedure, or the importance of policy and procedure. One of the numerous roles of supervisors is not only to enforce the policies and procedures of their organization, but also to make suggestions for improving or revising existing policies and procedures. To help equip supervisors to make recommendations for revision of existing policies and procedures, we will examine the importance of policy and procedure, what it is and what it is not intended to do.

Organizational Structure

The design of the organizational structure and management system is an important aspect of management. Organizational structure provides the basic tool for accomplishing stated purposes and objectives. Management systems establish the general courses of management action to ensure efficient coordination. Adherence to sound management principles and behavioral considerations are fundamental to the design of a management system (Chang and Campo-Flores, 1980).

For example, the organizational structure will be different for a probation agency than for a maximum-security prison. Consequently, there will be different policies, procedures, and mission statements, as well. Moreover, the management system probably will differ due to the inherent lack of similarities between the two agencies. A prison will have more layers in its management system (sergeants, lieu-tenants, captains, majors, deputy wardens, and the warden) than a probation office (usually a unit supervisor and an administrator). Regardless of the agency you work for and its management system, it is very important to follow the agency's estab-lished policies and procedures to ensure a well-run organization.

Policies and Procedures Provide Guidance

To effectively manage any organization, the implementation of sound policies and procedures is mandatory. Policy and procedures give employees guidelines on how to perform their job. Without established policies and procedures, it would be virtually impossible for any organization to achieve its goals and objectives. It is the supervisor's job to know the policies and procedures, review them with the line staff, and gain their compliance.

Ongoing Review of Policies and Procedures

You and your staff should review policies and procedures on an ongoing basis to ensure that they are still applicable and necessary. Sometimes, it is necessary to revise existing policy and procedures to reflect actual practices (Drapkin, 1996). Policies and procedures should cover all aspects of your organization. When there are new situations, such as for sick call, for special inmate programs, or for any other circumstances, new policies and procedures need to be written and approved so they can be put in place. Having such policies and procedures relieves the guess-work on how to proceed.

Importance of Policies and Procedure

Policies and procedures are a necessary aspect of sound management principles for the following reasons:

1. Policy statements state what is to be done. For example, "It is the policy of this agency that all inmates are to be searched before entering this facility."

2. Procedures tell the employee how to carry out the policy statement, in other words: 1) inmates are told to empty out their pockets, 2) inmates are told to place their hands on the wall, 3) an officer of the same gender as the inmate will search the inmate, and so forth.

3. Policies and procedures give employees guidelines on how to do their job.

4. Policies and procedures help ensure uniformity in the performance of the job among all shifts.

5. Policies and procedures help negate lawsuits. If an employee is acting within the scope of the established policies and procedures, litigation is reduced, and the agency's success against any litigation that is brought is enhanced.

6. Policies and procedures are necessary to receive accreditation from the American Correctional Association.

7. Policies and procedures protect employees. If an employee is acting within the scope of the established polices and procedures, the employee cannot be disciplined by a supervisor who might be "out to get" that employee.

8. Policies and procedures help supervisors perform their job. If an employee is not following the established policies and procedures, supervisors are justified in implementing discipline.

9. Policies and procedures tell all employees what they can and cannot do. If there is any question concerning an aspect of their job, employees can turn to the policy and procedures manual for guidance.

10. Finally, policies and procedures enhance the professionalism of an organization.

Because of the importance of policies and procedures, they should be explained to all employees at the beginning of their employment and then reviewed periodically with the supervisor throughout the year. All employees should have the opportunity to make suggestions for the revision of existing policies and the implementation of new policies, as needed.

Employees should sign an acknowledgment form stating that they have read and understand the policy and procedures manual of their agency. It is not a good idea to have them state in writing that they agree to abide by the policies and procedures of their agency, as this can be construed as an implied contractual agreement in some states. With an implied, or actual contractual agreement, it is more difficult to impose discipline. In this case, you usually would have to show an intent to violate the contract on the part of the employee. Furthermore, with a contract, there is less room to add the phrase "other duties, as required" to a job description. A contract will tie down too many specifics in regards to a basic job description. For the same reason, it is not a good idea to give all employees their own copy of the policy and procedures manual; rather, they should have access to one when they request it.

Remember, a policy and procedures manual is a guideline. It provides guidance on what personnel action you can take, when necessary. But, the policy manual will do you no good if you do not review it with your staff members and make recommendations for revisions, when this becomes necessary.

9 KNOW THE LAW

Throughout this book, we have examined various traits and skills that all supervisors should know and practice. We have examined the various roles that you will be expected to fulfill as a supervisor. We now will look at yet another role that you will have to fulfill: being familiar with the various laws that affect employer-employee relationships.

There are numerous laws that affect the employer-employee relationship. Some are federal, some state, and some local. We will examine some of the more common federal ones so that you at least will have a working knowledge of them. The information in this chapter is for informational use and is not intended to be a legal opinion or the interpretation of any existing laws. Hopefully, your organization will have legal counsel for you and your administration if there are questions that arise pertaining to these or other employer-employee type of laws.

Americans with Disabilities Act

The Americans with Disabilities Act (ADA) was enacted to prevent discrimination against any person because of an actual or perceived disability that the individual has. Furthermore, the employer might have to make special accommodations for a potential employee who is protected by the ADA. Simply stated, this law implies that if persons can perform the basic functions of the job they applied for, but need special accommodations, they cannot be discriminated against or denied employment simply for that reason. The special accommodations must be reasonable under this act.

Age Discrimination in Employment Act

The Age Discrimination in Employment Act of 1967 (ADEA) prohibits discrimination in the employment relationship based on an employee's age. You cannot ask prospective employees their age; however, if there is an age requirement for the job, such as twenty-one, you may ask them if they are at least twenty-one. You also need to inform them that there is a minimum-age requirement for the job and that is why you asked them if they were at least twenty-one.

In other words, under the ADEA, an employer cannot force a person to retire or set minimum mandatory retirement ages. An employer, however, can offer voluntary retirement programs once an employee is a certain age and has worked a certain number of years. Additionally, if older employees want to take advantage of an early retirement-incentive program, they must sign a waiver form, which relinquishes their right to sue their employer under the provisions of the ADEA.

The ADEA has other aspects to it besides abolishment of a mandatory retirement age. As a first-line supervisor, you cannot discriminate in favor of employees in this protected group by giving them a safe or easy assignment because of their age. If employees are fit for duty, they are expected to perform their job as required by existing standards. If employees cannot perform the basic functions of their job, you need to initiate retraining or discipline, as appropriate.

If you do have older employees, who cannot perform the basic aspects of the job, take the necessary action. Do not treat them differently than a younger employee who cannot perform the basic functions of the job. Do not, under any circumstance, make reference to the fact that the individuals are older employees, suggest that they should retire, or even hint that "perhaps they cannot do the job because of their age." If you do, they will have an excellent claim of discrimination under the provisions of the ADEA.

Dress and Grooming Standards

Can you require male employees to have their hair a certain length, and perhaps not have a restriction on the length of female's hair? Yes. However, if you do adopt different dress and grooming standards for male and female employees, make sure that the policy is equally enforced and it is not demeaning to one gender.

Additionally, make sure there is a justified, articulated reason for the different dress and grooming policy.

Obviously, adopting dress and grooming standards for corrections professionals is standard business practice. It can be argued that requiring men's hair to be collar length and female's hair to be in a "bun" or "pinned-up" and above-the-collar-length is necessary as a safety precaution. Long hair is something that an inmate can grab and use to assault the officer. However, adopting the same hair-length requirement in a probation agency might be more difficult as the safety reason is not as imminent in a probation setting.

References

On the issue of references, if you have employees who are below-standard performers, had disciplinary problems, caused disruptions in the workplace and quit, can you tell their prospective employers the truth about their employment with your agency? The answer is maybe. You only can state facts about the employees' past job performances. A fact is something that you can prove without question. The fact that they received low scores on their performance evaluations or were disciplined under certain circumstances could be revealed. The rule to follow is to refer all employment reference checks on current and former employees to the personnel or human resources department.

If you release inaccurate information concerning employees' job performances, you could be sued for libel or slander. Generally speaking, slander is a spoken falsehood and libel is a written falsehood. To achieve a successful suit, this information must be false and be knowingly communicated to a third party with the intent to defame the person to whom you are referring.

In the situation of employees who quit, had poor performance evaluations, and discipline problems, suppose the poor evaluation that you gave them was upgraded on appeal, or the disciplinary action taken against them was modified on appeal, and you told the prospective employers how bad those employees were? The information that you gave, although you believed it to be true, might be considered injurious to the employees if they did not get the job because of your statements. Consequently, the ex-employees might have grounds for libel or slander suits. Also, do not talk off the record to another employer regarding a current or former employee's job performance. Whatever you say in your role as supervisor is on the record.

The best rule to follow, to protect yourself and your agency against a potential libel suit, is to not release any information about employees to a third party except: job title, job description, length of employment, and rate of pay. Any other information should not be released, unless you have a signed, notarized statement from the employees authorizing you to release additional information pertaining to their employment. Then, only release the information that is factual after consulting with your personnel department or agency lawyer.

Family Medical Leave Act

The Family Medical Leave Act (FMLA) of 1993 allows qualified employees to take a leave of absence for up to twelve weeks to attend to a family emergency. The leave is generally without pay, but employees' insurance coverage is continued, and they are guaranteed their job upon their return to work. Basically, the FMLA works as follows:

1. An eligible employee (one who has been employed for twelve consecutive months) needs time off from work to attend to a lengthy family emergency that is medically necessary.

2. The emergency can be to tend to a sick relative who lives with the employee, such as the employee's spouse, for the birth of a child, the adoption of a child, or other qualifying medical reasons.

3. There must be a written statement from a medical doctor stating what the emergency is and for how long it might last.

4. The amount of leave an employee may take is twelve weeks in a twelve-month period.

5. The employee may use any earned compensatory time, vacations days, holidays, and sick days during the twelve-week FMLA leave to guard against loss of pay. Once the employee's earned paid time off has been exhausted, the remainder of the leave is without pay.

6. Once employees return to work, they must be reinstated in their current job, or a comparable job at a comparable rate of pay and with comparable benefits.

This law was enacted to safeguard employees' jobs, if they are required to take an extensive period of time off from their job due to a medical emergency. However, the employer has rights under the FMLA too, such as:

- The employer may require the employee to provide medical documentation prior to the leave beginning and at thirty-day intervals during the leave.

- The employer may require the employee to produce written notification from the doctor that the employee is able to return to work.

- The employee is still an employee while on FMLA leave. Therefore, any violations the employee commits may be dealt with accordingly. For example, if the supervisor contacts employees and informs them that they need documentation to verify the FMLA leave, and the employees refuse to comply with such a request, this could be considered insubordination to a supervisor, and should be handled accordingly.

- The FMLA does not grant employees greater rights than they already have. All they are guaranteed is their job or a comparable job with comparable pay and benefits.

OSHA

The Occupational Safety and Health Act, which created the Occupational Safety and Health Administration (OSHA), protects workers. OSHA sets forth guidelines that employers must follow to ensure a safe workplace. Additionally, OSHA officials may conduct inspections of the workplace to ensure compliance with their safety standards. A typical OSHA inspection would ensure that all mechanical equipment is working properly, safety equipment is in good working condition, and that there are no apparent hazards that could cause injury to employees.

Theft

Employee theft is a problem faced by all employers, even those in the field of corrections. As a supervisor, you have an obligation to prevent employee theft, but you must do so in the right manner, in accordance with applicable laws.

There are ways to combat employee theft. The two most common ways are by searches of employees, their lockers and their personal belongings, and by electronic surveillance. Both methods employ a somewhat aggressive stance to proactively combat employee theft and should be discussed with legal counsel prior to actually implementing them.

Basically, after conferring with legal counsel, if you implement either searches of employees or use surveillance cameras, the following should be considered:

1. *Searches.* Make sure you communicated verbally and in writing, that all employees, their lockers, and the personal belongings that they bring to

work, may be searched at anytime. You should have a policy in place to control the scope of the searches and what to do with any illegal or contraband property that may be found in their possession.

2. *Surveillance Cameras.* Communicate to employees verbally and in writing that they may be monitored by surveillance cameras. Cameras should not be placed in locations that are overly intrusive or that could compromise an employee's right to reasonable privacy, such as locker rooms or bathrooms.

Sexual Harassment

Another area of the law to which supervisors need to pay particular attention is that of sexual harassment. Sexual harassment is no joking matter, and all complaints concerning sexual harassment must be investigated. Failure of the supervisor to conduct an investigation into allegations of sexual harassment could give the impression that the supervisor condones such action. This, in turn, could give the complainant justification to pursue the matter further, because the inaction of the supervisor to take reasonable action to prevent sexual harassment, in effect, is creating a hostile work environment.

Essentially, sexual harassment is any unwelcome sexual advances, requests for sexual favors, and other verbal or physical conduct of a sexual nature when the submission to such conduct is made explicitly or implicitly a term of an individual's employment, or the submission to or rejection of such conduct by an individual is used to give that individual preferential or adverse treatment, or if the conduct unreasonably interferes with the normal conduct of business or creates a hostile work environment.

The best way to combat sexual harassment is to have a policy that defines what sexual harassment is and that prohibits this type of action. Additionally, there must be training for supervisors in ways to recognize sexual harassment. Appropriate action must be taken on all complaints alleging sexual harassment. Furthermore, the policy forbidding sexual harassment should make it clear that a person will be able to make a complaint of sexual harassment without fear of retaliation from others.

Remember that the aggressor in a sexual harassment complaint is not always a male. It is possible for a female to sexually harass a male. Likewise, persons of the same gender also can harass each other sexually.

Sex Discrimination

Sex discrimination is not the same as sexual harassment. The Equal Employment Opportunity Commission (EEOC) guidelines on discrimination because of sex enumerate several practices of employers that lead to sex discrimination:

1. Refusal to hire a woman because of assumptions of the comparative employment characteristics of women in general

2. Refusal to hire an individual (male or female) based on a stereotypical characteristic of the sexes

3. Restrictions or prohibitions against the employment of married women where there is not a corresponding restriction on prohibition against the employment of married men

4. Labeling jobs as men's jobs or women's jobs

5. Differences between men and women with regard to fringe benefits or pay

Your job is to ensure that job assignments are made solely on the basis of ability, not gender. The only exception might be that only officers of the same gender as the offender may search an offender.

Immigration Reform

The Immigration Reform and Control Law of 1986 was implemented to prevent the hiring of illegal immigrants. It is a violation of this law to knowingly hire, recruit, or refer for a fee any alien not authorized to work in the United States. This is why applicants must complete an I-9 Form, which states that they are citizens of the United States, or are here legally and are authorized to work.

Substance Abuse Tests

Another area of the law that affects the employer-employee relationship is that of drug and alcohol testing. Most companies and agencies require applicants to submit to a postoffer drug and alcohol test. Furthermore, several agencies or private correctional companies have a requirement of annual, random, or for-cause drug or alcohol tests of employees.

There should be a written and published alcohol and drug policy that is communicated to all current employees and job applicants. These policies should explain employee rights in the workplace and be clear enough to discourage a drug or alcohol abuser from joining your staff. As a general rule, policies should be implemented that make the use, possession, sale, or distribution of alcohol or drugs while on duty or on company property cause for immediate termination. Furthermore, employees involved in any on-the-job accident should be tested for alcohol or drug abuse.

There also needs to be an Employee Assistance Program (EAP) available for employees who abuse alcohol or drugs, so that they can receive help in overcoming their addiction. The EAP should be available to employees who are referred by management, or by self-referral. Referral to an EAP should not be held against the employee.

Violence

The final area of the law that we will look at is that of violence in the workplace. Employees have the right to feel safe and secure in the workplace and should be able to perform their jobs without fear of becoming a victim of workplace violence. Therefore, agencies should have a policy in place to help reduce the likelihood of workplace violence.

However, there are some practical steps that can be taken to help reduce the likelihood of workplace violence:

1. There must be a careful screening of all applicants.

2. There should be a written policy prohibiting any overt acts of violence, threats of violence, or intimidation.

3. All reports of workplace violence must be investigated and appropriate action taken.

4. There should be an Employee Assistance Program available where employees may go or be referred to for anger control.

5. Supervisors should be aware of the characteristics that are common in a workplace violence perpetrator (generally speaking): white male with a history of drug or alcohol abuse who has difficulty accepting authority. He threatens fellow employees and has a history of violence. However, supervisors should be aware that anyone of any race, and females, as well as males, may become violent. With this knowledge, supervisors should take proactive steps to prevent the occurrence of workplace violence

(Flentje, Farha and Smith, 1995). These proactive steps include steps 1-4, listed previously.

6. Once employees are terminated from employment, or resign in bad standing, they should not be allowed on company property unescorted.

After reading this chapter, you might think that you need to be a lawyer to be an effective supervisor. Luckily, you do not, but you do need to be familiar with the various laws that affect the employer-employee relationship. Furthermore, you will want to communicate the various laws to your employees. They, too, need to have a basic understanding of the various laws that affect their working relationship with you. Additionally, you should keep abreast of current laws that affect the employer-employee relationship.

10 Conclusion

Throughout this book, we have examined the various roles that you, as a supervisor, must fulfill. The topics that were covered in this book are the topics that this author wishes, in hindsight, someone would have told him about when he first became a supervisor several years ago.

Since everyone is different, your supervisory style probably will not be the same as the supervisory style of your previous supervisor. It is imperative that you determine what your supervisory style is and work with it. There are supervisory inventories that you can take to help you determine your supervisory style, or perhaps you were able to determine your supervisory style after reading Chapter One. Supervisory inventories usually can be obtained through local community college bookstores, libraries, and by correspondence courses, including those available from the American Correctional Association.

When this author teaches supervisory classes to newly promoted supervisors and to employees who are eligible for promotion, he always starts his class by asking two questions: What characteristics make a good supervisor, and what characteristics make a bad supervisor? He then writes the students' answers on butcher-block paper and has them posted conspicuously throughout the instructional period. Listed below are some of the most common answers to these questions:

1. What are the traits of an effective supervisor?
   a. Fair
   b. Consistent
   c. Follows the rules
   d. Knows the job of the people he or she is supervising
   e. Honest
   f. Does not talk down to line staff

2. What characteristics make an ineffective supervisor?
   a. Plays favorites
   b. Thinks the rules do not apply to him or her
   c. Talks down to line staff
   d. Is not fair. If one of his or her "favorites" gets in trouble, the bad supervisor protects him or her.
   e. Is not consistent/is moody

The reason this author asks these questions and posts the answers on the wall is for the participants to actually "see" the characteristics of a good and bad supervisor. Furthermore, these same characteristics can be transferred to line staff when they supervise inmates or a probation caseload, because if they supervise inmates, they are a supervisor! Line staff may not realize it, but these characteristics should apply to them, too, in their working relationship with inmates.

You can learn a great deal from observing other supervisors. You will want to emulate good supervisors. This author learned his best lessons by observing a bad supervisor. This author observed that whatever he did, the author would basically do the exact opposite. He fit all of the "bad characteristics," and he gained a lack of respect from his employees. Therefore, this author made it a point to be fair, consistent, and by-the-book in his dealings with line staff.

Make sure that you are well equipped to handle the supervisory challenges that will come your way. If you treat all employees fairly, you will have very few problems with them. That is not to say you should treat all employees the same, because you cannot. You, however, must treat all employees fairly and be consistent in dealing with their problems.

You might think that an employee's complaint about a particular matter is trivial, and maybe it is. However, to those employees, their complaint is a real problem that needs attention. They will expect you to handle it in some manner. If employees quit coming to you with their problems, you might want to stop and reflect on how you have been handling their problems. Are they no longer coming to you because there are no problems (which is not likely), or are they no longer coming to you because of the way you do, or do not, handle their problems?

In some aspects of your new job, you will need assistance and/or guidance from your supervisor. Make sure that when you conduct your first employee performance evaluation and interview, you get your supervisor's input to be sure that you have not overlooked anything. Remember, your evaluation of employees could affect their employment with your agency, so be honest and fair in your evaluations.

The same is true with your recommendations concerning discipline. Be sure that you have all of the facts before you make a recommendation to your supervisor concerning what appropriate discipline, if any, should be imposed. Make sure that you are following the established policies and procedures on discipline and that your recommendation is appropriate for the offense committed.

In responding to grievances, be sure that you have all of the facts before you make a decision. Allow grievants sufficient time to express their grievances to you. You will settle a large share of all grievances at your level if you allow the employees to express their grievances and you act concerned with their problem. Oftentimes, employees just wants to "get it off their chest" and talking to you about the problem makes them feel better.

If the grievance goes past your level, do not take it personally. There are some complaints that you cannot handle and that should go on to the next level. Just be prepared to give the reasons for your decision to the grievance board and conduct yourself in a professional manner.

In regards to policies and procedures, as a supervisor, if you think a policy needs to be changed, make the recommendation for the appropriate change. Do not complain about the policy to line staff, as this will convey the message to them that since you do not think the policy is important, they do not need to follow it. You are an extension of the administration, and employees will view *all* of your actions and statements as being sanctioned by the administration.

The following "Ten Commandments" will help you in becoming an efficient supervisor. However, you must follow them and make them a part of your supervisory philosophy.

As you move up the career ladder, you will learn that being a supervisor is a very rewarding job. You will have challenges, but by applying the knowledge you have acquired by reading this book, you will be able to face the challenges head on and come out on top. You now are in the position to make a difference for your employees and your organization. Make that difference a positive one!

Ten Commandments for Leader-managers

1. Make a commitment to being an effective leader

2. Establish a climate for change that will lead to higher levels of achievement

3. Formulate a clearly articulated vision of the future

4. Build a team of people who are jointly responsible for achieving the vision

5. Communicate the organizational values through your words and actions

6. Develop a strategy that will help you achieve the vision

7. Create a climate for authentic dialog

8. Motivate others by helping them move toward their ideal selves

9. Take a personal interest in the development of each of your people

10. Gauge progress on the basis of critical success factors (Hitt, 1988, p. 217)

BIBLIOGRAPHY

American Correctional Association. 1990. *Correctional Issues: Correctional Management.* Lanham, Maryland: American Correctional Association.

————. 1991a. *Correctional Supervision Correspondence Course.* Lanham, Maryland: American Correctional Association.

————. 1991b. *Correctional Mid-Management Skills Correspondence Course.* Lanham, Maryland: American Correctional Association.

————. 1993. *Understanding Cultural Diversity.* Lanham, Maryland: American Correctional Association.

————. 1998. *Current Concepts in Correctional Leadership.* Lanham, Maryland: American Correctional Association.

Ardis, Patrick M. and Michael J. Comer. 1987. *Risk Management, Computers, Fraud and Insurance.* United Kingdom: McGraw Hill Book Company (UK) Limited.

Bell, Arthur H. 1989. *The Complete Manger's Guide To Interviewing.* Homewood, Illinois: Dow Jones-Irwin.

Berk, Joseph and Susan Berk. 1991. *Managing Effectively.* New York: Sterling Publishing Company, Inc.

Blake, Robert R. and Jane S. Mouton. 1964. *The Managerial Grid.* Houston, Texas: Gulf Publishing Co.

Blanchard, Kenneth, Donald Carew, and Eunice Parisi-Carew. 1990. *The One Minute Manager Builds High Performing Teams.* New York: William Morrow and Company, Inc.

Broadwell, M. 1995 (September). Why Command and Control Won't Go Away. *Training.* Atlanta: Lakewood Publications.

Carlisle, Kenneth E., Ph.D. and Sheila E. Murphy, Ph.D. 1986. *Practical Motivation Handbook.* New York: John Wiley and Sons.

Chang, Y. N. and Filemon Campo-Flores. 1980. *Business Policy and Strategy.* Santa Monica, California: Goodyear Publishing, Inc.

Clemmer, J. 1995. *Pathways to Performance.* Rockland, California: Prima Publishing.

Collins, William. 1997. *Correctional Law for the Correctional Officer.* Lanham, Maryland: American Correctional Association.

Creech, Bill. 1994. *The Five Pillars Of TQM.* Dutton, New York: Truman Talley Books.

Drapkin, Martin. 1996. *Developing Policies and Procedures for Jails: A Step-by-Step Guide.* Lanham, Maryland: American Correctional Association.

Drucker, Peter F. 1966. *The Effective Executive.* New York: Harper and Row.

Eims, Larry. 1975. *Be The Leader You Were Meant To Be.* Wheaton, Illinois: Victor Books.

Ferris, Gerald R., Sherman D. Rosen, and Darold T. Barnum. 1995. *Handbook of Human Resource Management.* Cambridge, Massachusetts: Blackwell Publishers.

Flentje, Gloria, G. Farha, and Susan L. Smith. 1995. *How To Avoid Legal Pitfalls in Hiring in Kansas.* Nashville, Tennessee: M. Lee Smith Publishers and Printers, Inc.

Germane, Gaylen E. 1986. *The Executive Course.* Reading, Massachusetts: Addison Wesley Publishing Company, Inc.

Greene, Mark R. 1981. *Insurance and Risk Management for Small Business, Third Edition.* Washington, D.C.: U.S. Government Printing Office.

Heyel, Carl. 1973. *The Encyclopedia of Management, Second Edition.* New York: Von Nostrand Reinhold Company.

Hitt, William D. 1988. *The Leader-Manager.* Columbus, Ohio: Battle Press.

Holpp, L. 1995 (March). If Empowerment Is So Good, Why Does it Hurt? *Training.* Atlanta: Lakewood Publications.

Juran, J. 1989. *Juran on Leadership for Quality: An Executive Handbook.* New York: The Free Press.

Klubanik, Joan P. 1995. *Rewarding and Recognizing Employees.* Chicago: Irwin Professional Publishing.

Lawler III, Edward E., Susan Albers Mohrman, and Gerald E. Ledford, Jr. 1992. *Employee Involvement and Total Quality Management.* San Francisco: Jossey-Bass.

Lynch, Richard. 1993. *Lead!.* San Francisco: Jossey-Bass.

McAnany, Van Cleave and P. A. Phillips. 1995. Employment and Workers' Compensation Law Seminar. Kansas City, Kansas. July.

McGregor, Douglas. 1960. *The Human Side Of Enterprise.* New York: McGraw Hill.

Mondy, R. Wayne, Arthur Sharplin, and Shane R. Premeaux. *Managment Concepts, Practices and Skills.* Needham Heights, Massachusetts: Allyn and Bacon.

Mumma, Frederick S., Ed.D. 1992. What Makes Your Team Tick? Organization Design and Development, Inc.

National Institute of Business Management, Inc. *Creating and Motivating a Superior, Loyal Staff.* New York: National Institute of Business Management.

Patten, Thomas H. Jr. 1982. *A Manager's Guide to Performance Appraisal.* New York: The Free Press.

Peters, T. 1992. *Liberation Management.* New York: Alfred A. Knopf.

Raddle, Paul O. 1981. *Supervising.* Austin, Texas: Learning Concepts.

Roberts, Albert R. 1989. *Juvenile Justice Policies, Programs and Services.* Chicago: The Dorsey Press

Rosen, Robert H. 1996. *Leading People.* New York: Penguin Group.

Sashkin, M. and Kenneth J. Kiser. 1993. *Putting Total Quality Management to Work*. San Francisco: Berret-Koehler Publishers.

Stamps, D. 1996 (March). A Piece of the Action. *Training*. Atlanta: Lakewood Publications.

Swan, William S., Ph.D. 1991. *How To Do A Superior Performance Evaluation*. New York: John Wiley and Sons, Inc.

Viscounti, Ron and Marty Brounstein. 1992. *Effective Recruiting Strategies*. Los Altos, California: Crisp Publications, Inc.

Yate, Martin John. 1987. *Hiring The Best*. Boston, Massachusetts: Bob Adams, Inc.

INDEX

About the Author

Scott D. Hutton has more than seventeen years of experience in various criminal justice and law enforcement positions. Dr. Hutton was the Interim Administrator of the Wyandotte County Jail in Kansas City, Kansas, and the Administrator of the Wyandotte County Juvenile Detention Center in Kansas City, Kansas. Prior to this, he served as the Director of the Fourth Judicial District Community Corrections in Ottawa, Kansas and as the Supervisor with the Wyandotte County Community Corrections in Kansas City, Kansas. Before this, he was a police officer in Otturnwa, Iowa and Killeen, Texas. He also served in the United States Army. Currently, he is a Substance Abuse Account Manager with Roche Diagnostics.

In 1996, Dr. Hutton received his Ph.D. from La Salle University. He has a Master of Science degree and a Bachelor's degree from American Technological University. Additionally, he has attended numerous workshops and seminars on management issues. Dr. Hutton has taught college-level classes on probation and law enforcement.